SHOW WHAT YOU KNOW® ON THE

OAT
FOR GRADE 6

READING

grade 6

**PREPARATION FOR THE
OHIO ACHIEVEMENT TESTS**

Show What You Know® Publishing

NAME

Published by:
Show What You Know® Publishing
A Division of Englefield & Associates, Inc.
P.O. Box 341348
Columbus, OH 43234-1348
Phone: 614-764-1211
www.showwhatyouknowpublishing.com
www.passtheoat.com

Copyright © 2006 by Englefield & Associates, Inc.

All rights reserved. No part of this book, including interior design, cover design, and icons, may be reproduced or transmitted in any form, by any means (electronic, photocopying, recording, or otherwise), without the prior written permission of the publisher.

Printed in the United States of America
08 07 06   20 19 18 17 16 15 14 13 12 11 10 9 8 7 6 5 4 3 2 1

ISBN: 1-59230-168-1

Limit of Liability/Disclaimer of Warranty: The authors and publishers have used their best efforts in preparing this book. Englefield & Associates, Inc., and the authors make no representations or warranties with respect to the contents of this book and specifically disclaim any implied warranties and shall in no event be liable for any loss of any kind including but not limited to special, incidental, consequential, or other damages.

Acknowledgements

Show What You Know® Publishing acknowledges the following for their efforts in making this assessment material available for Ohio students, parents, and teachers.

Cindi Englefield, President/Publisher
Eloise Boehm-Sasala, Vice President/Managing Editor
Erin McDonald, Project Editor
Christine Filippetti, Project Editor
Jill Borish, Project Editor
Heather Holliday, Project Editor
Charles V. Jackson, Project Editor
Lauren Lipaj, Contributor
Jennifer Harney, Illustrator/Cover Designer

About the Contributors

The content of this book was written BY teachers FOR teachers and students and was designed specifically for the Ohio Achievement Test (OAT) for Grade 6 Reading. Contributions to the Reading chapter of this book were also made by the educational publishing staff at Show What You Know® Publisihing. Dr. Jolie S. Brams, a clinical child and family psychologist, is the contributing author of the Test Anxiety and Test-Taking Strategies chapters of this book. Without the contributions of these people, this book would not be possible.

Table of Contents

Introduction v

Test Anxiety 1

Test-Taking Strategies 11

Understanding the OAT for Grade 6 Reading 21
    Introduction 21
    Questions I Will Answer on the OAT 22
    Item Distribution on the OAT for Grade 6 Reading 26
    Scoring 26
    Additional Information 28
    Glossary 29

Reading Tutorial 35
    Directions for Reading Tutorial 35
    Reading Tutorial 36

Reading Practice Test 1 109
    Directions for Reading Practice Test 1 109
    Reading Practice Test 1 110
    Reading Practice Test 1: Answer Document 128

Reading Practice Test 2 135
    Directions for Reading Practice Test 2 135
    Reading Practice Test 2 136
    Reading Practice Test 2: Answer Document 151

Introduction

Introduction

The purpose of the Ohio Achievement Test (OAT) is to measure student learning. Throughout the school year, students are exposed to a wide variety of concepts from a range of subjects, only some of which are tested by the Reading OAT. Yet it is important that all Ohio Academic Content Standards be taught in order to ensure that students have a well-rounded understanding of the sixth-grade curriculum. Students who have been taught the elements of this curriculum will have been exposed to all that is assessed by the Reading OAT. Nonetheless, students will benefit from the review of key details as they prepare to take this assessment.

The *Show What You Know® on the OAT for Grade 6 Reading, Student Workbook* is designed to help students better understand the types of information they will see on the Reading OAT. This book will help students review important elements assessed by the Reading OAT; it is not a substitute for continuous teaching and learning, which take place both in and outside the classroom. But, as with any assessment, it is a good idea to review principles that have been taught and learned prior to taking the Reading OAT.

It is impossible to cover everything students have learned throughout their life in one book. However, students can use this book to refresh their memory and to brush up on their test-taking skills. This book is full of practice questions, test-taking hints, and problem-solving strategies—all of which were designed to help students show what they know. *Show What You Know® on the OAT for Grade 6 Reading, Student Workbook* includes many features that will benefit students as they prepare for the OAT:

- The first two chapters—Test Anxiety and Test-Taking Strategies—were written especially for sixth-grade students. Test Anxiety offers advice on how to reduce anxious feelings about tests, and Test-Taking Strategies offers helpful tips they can use to do their best on tests.

- The Reading Tutorial chapter of this book contains introductory material about the test, including Item Distribution and Scoring Information. The Reading Tutorial contains informational and literary passages. After each reading passage, students will answer multiple-choice, short-answer, and extended-response questions. A sample Answer Document page is located next to the question to help students become familiar with how to write their answer in the space allowed. An analysis for each tutorial question is given to help students identify the correct answer.

- The Reading Practice Test chapters of this book each contain one 40-question practice test and an Answer Document. The reading passages are informational and literary, and the questions are multiple-choice, short-answer, and extended-response.

For easy reference, this Student Workbook correlates with the *Show What You Know® on the OAT for Grade 6 Reading, Parent/Teacher Supplement* (sold separately).

Good luck on the OAT!

Test Anxiety

What is Test Anxiety?

Test anxiety is just a fancy name for "feeling nervous about tests." Everyone knows what it is like to be nervous. Feeling nervous is not a good experience!

Lots of students have anxiety about taking tests, so if you are a test worrier, don't let it worry you! Most likely, many of your fellow students and friends also have fearful feelings about tests but do not share these feelings with others. Sixth grade is a time when everyone wants to seem "grown up," and few sixth graders want to look weak or afraid in the eyes of their friends or their teachers. But not talking to others about anxiety only makes the situation worse. It makes you feel alone and also makes you wonder if there is something "wrong" with you. Be brave! Talk to your friends and teachers about test anxiety. You will feel better for sharing.

What Does It Feel Like to Have Test Anxiety?

Students who have test anxiety don't always feel the same way, but they always feel bad! Here are some ways that students feel when they are anxious about tests.

- **Students who have test anxiety rarely think good things about themselves.**
  They lack confidence in their abilities, and they are convinced they will do poorly on tests. Not only do they feel bad about themselves and their abilities, but they just can't keep negative thoughts out of their minds! They would probably make terrible detectives, because in spite of all the good things they could find out about themselves, they only think about what they can't do. And that's not the worst of it! Students with test anxiety also exaggerate. When they think of the smallest problem, it becomes a hundred times bigger, especially when they think about tests. They are very unforgiving of themselves. If they make a mistake, they always think the worst or exaggerate the situation. If they do poorly on a quiz, they never say, "Well, it's just a quiz, and I'll try better next time." Instead they think, "That test was terrible and I can only imagine how badly I'll do next week." For students with test anxiety, there is never a brighter day ahead. They don't think many good thoughts about themselves, and they certainly don't have a happy outlook on their lives.

- **Students who have test anxiety have poor "thinking habits."**
  Negative thinking is a habit just like any other habit. Some habits are good and some habits are bad, but negative thinking is probably the worst habit of all. A habit forms when you do something over and over again until it becomes so much a part of you that you don't think about it anymore. Students with test anxiety develop negative ways of thinking about themselves and about schoolwork, especially about tests. They tend to make the worst out of situations and imagine all kinds of possibilities that probably will not happen. Their thoughts grow like a mushroom out of control! Besides having negative ideas about tests, they begin to have negative ideas about most everything else in their lives. This is not a good way of thinking because the more poorly they feel about themselves, the worse they do in school, and bad grades make them feel even worse about themselves. What a mess! Students who have constant negative thoughts about themselves and schoolwork probably have test anxiety.

- **Students who have test anxiety may feel physically uncomfortable or even ill.**
  It is important to know that your mind and body are connected! What goes on in your mind can change how your body feels, and how your body feels can influence what goes on in your thinking. When students have test anxiety, their thoughts might cause them to have physical symptoms which include a fast heartbeat, butterflies in the stomach, headaches, and all sorts of other physical problems. Some kids become so ill they end up going to the doctor because they believe they are truly sick. Some students miss a lot of school due to anxiety, but they aren't really ill. Instead, their

thoughts are controlling their bodies in a negative way. Some anxious students do not realize that what they are feeling is anxiety. They miss many days of school, not because they are lazy or neglectful, but because they believe they truly are not feeling well. Unfortunately, the more school they miss, the more behind they are and the more nervous they feel. Students who suffer from test anxiety probably feel even worse on test days. Their uncomfortable physical feelings will make them either avoid the test completely or feel so bad during the test that they do poorly. Guess what happens then. They feel even worse about themselves, become more anxious, and the cycle goes on and on.

- **Students who have test anxiety "freak out" and want to escape.**
  Many students feel so bad when they are anxious that they will do anything to avoid that feeling. For most students, this means running away from problems, especially tests. Some students try to get away from tests by missing school. This does not solve any problems; the more a student is away from school, the harder schoolwork is, and the worse he or she feels. Some students worry about being worried! It may sound silly, but they are worried that they are going to freak out, and guess what happens . . . they do! They are so terrified that they will have uncontrollable anxious feelings that they actually get anxious feelings when thinking about this problem! For many students, anxiety is such a bad feeling that they will do anything not to feel anxious, even if it means failing tests or school. Although they know this will cause them problems in the future, their anxiety is so overwhelming they would rather avoid anxiety now and fail later. Unfortunately, this is usually what happens.

- **Students who have test anxiety do not show what they know on tests.**
  Students who have test anxiety do not make good decisions on tests. Instead of focusing their thoughts, planning out their answers, and using what they know, students find themselves "blanking out." They stare at the paper, and no answer is there! They become "stuck" and cannot move on. Some students come up with the wrong answers because their anxiety gets in the way of reading directions carefully and thinking about answers thoughtfully. Their minds are running in a hundred different ways and none of those ways seem to be getting them anywhere. They forget to use what they know, and they also forget to use study skills that can help them do their best. When students are so worried that they cannot make good decisions and use all of the talents they have, it is called test anxiety.

Are You One of These "Test-Anxious" Sixth Graders?

As you have seen, students with test anxiety have negative thoughts about themselves, often feel anxious to the point of being ill, freak out and want to escape, and rarely show what they know on tests. Do any of the following kids remind you of yourself?

Stay-Away Stephanie
Stephanie's thoughts tell her it is better to stay away from challenges, especially tests. Stephanie is a good girl, but she is always in trouble at school for avoiding tests. Sometimes, she really feels ill and begs her mom to allow her to stay home on test days. At other times, Stephanie does anything to avoid school, refusing to get up in the morning or to leave the house to catch the bus. Stephanie truly believes there is nothing worse than taking a test. She is so overwhelmed with anxiety that she forgets about the problems that will happen when she stays away from her responsibilities. Unfortunately, the more she stays away, the worse the situation becomes. Stay-Away Stephanie feels less nervous when she doesn't face a test, but she never learns to face her fears.

Worried Wendy
Wendy is the type of sixth grader who always expects the worst thing to happen. She has many negative thoughts. Even when situations have turned out to be OK, Wendy focuses on the few bad things that happened. She exaggerates negative events and forgets about everything good. Her mind races a mile a minute with all sorts of thoughts and ideas about tests. The more she thinks, the worse she feels, and her problems become unbelievably huge. Instead of just worrying about a couple of difficult questions on a test, she finds herself thinking about failing the whole test, being made fun of by her friends, being grounded by her parents, and never going to college. She completely forgets that her parents would never be so strict, that her friends like her for many more reasons than her test grades, and that she has all sorts of career choices ahead of her. No one is going to hold it against her if she performs poorly on a test. It is not going to ruin her life. However, Wendy believes all of that would happen. Her negative thoughts get in the way of thinking anything positive.

Critical Chris
Chris is the type of sixth grader who spends all of his time putting himself down. No matter what happens, he always feels he has been a failure. While some people hold grudges against others, Chris holds grudges against himself. No matter what little mistakes he makes, he can never forget them. Chris has had many good things happen to him in his life, and he has been successful many times. Unfortunately, Chris forgets all the good and only remembers the bad. Because he doesn't appreciate himself, Chris has test anxiety.

Victim Vince
Most sixth graders find it is important to take responsibility for their actions. It helps them understand that adulthood is just around the corner, and that they are smarter and more able than they ever thought they were. However, Vince is not like this. He can't take responsibility for himself at all. He thinks everything is someone else's fault and constantly complains about friends, parents, schoolwork, and especially tests. He tells himself, "They make those tests too hard." He sees the teachers as unfair, and he thinks life is generally against him. Vince does not feel there is anything he can do to help his situation, and there is little he thinks he can do to help himself with tests. Because he does not try to learn test-taking skills or to understand why he is afraid, he continues to feel hopeless and angry. Not surprisingly, he does poorly on tests, which only makes his thoughts about the world around him worse.

Perfect Pat
Everyone knows that there is more homework and responsibility in sixth grade than in previous grades. Everyone in the sixth grade needs to try his or her best, but no one should try as much as Pat does. All Pat does is worry. No matter what she does, it's never good enough. She will write book reports over and over and study for tests until she is exhausted. Trying hard is fine, but no matter what Pat does, she feels she has never done enough. Because she never accomplishes what she sets out to do (that would be impossible!), she worries all the time. Her anxiety level gets higher and higher. The more anxious she becomes, the worse she does on tests. This just makes her study and worry more. What a terrible situation!

How Do I Handle Test Anxiety?

Test anxiety is a very powerful feeling that convinces students they are weak and helpless. Feelings of test anxiety can be so powerful it seems there is nothing you can do to stop them. Anxiety seems to take over your mind and body and leaves you feeling like you are going to lose the test anxiety battle for sure.

The good news is that there are many simple things you can do to win the battle over test anxiety! If you can learn these skills in the sixth grade, you are on the road to success in school and for all other challenges in your life.

- **Change the way you think.**
  Most of us don't "think about how we think." We just go along thinking our thoughts and never really considering whether they are helpful or not helpful or if they are right or wrong. We rarely realize how much the way we think has to do with how well we get along in life. Our thoughts can influence how we feel about ourselves, how we get along with other people, how well we do in school, and how we perform on tests.

- **The Soda Pop Test.**
Most sixth graders have heard a parent or teacher tell them, "There is more than one side to any story." One student reported that his grandfather used to say, "There's more than one way to paint a fence." Have you ever considered how you think about different situations? Most situations can be looked at in many ways, both good and bad.

Take a can of soda pop and put it on your desk or dresser at home. Get out a piece of paper and a pen or a pencil. Now, draw a line down the middle of the paper. On one side, put a heading: "All the bad things about this can of soda pop." On the other side put another heading: "All the good things about this can of soda pop." If you think about that can of soda pop, you might come up with the following chart.

All the bad things about this can of soda pop	All the good things about this can of soda pop
Not an attractive color	Easy-to-read lettering
It's getting warm	Nice to have something to drink
Not much in the can	Inexpensive
Has a lot of sugar	Recyclable aluminum cans

Look how easy it is to write down good things or bad things about a silly can of soda pop! That can of soda pop is not really good or bad, it's just a can of soda pop, but we can either look at it in a positive way or we can think about everything negative that comes to our minds. Doesn't the same thing hold true for tests? Tests are not good or bad in themselves. Tests are just a way to challenge us and see what we know. Challenges can be stressful, but they can also be rewarding. Studying for tests can be boring and can take up a lot of free time, but we can also learn a lot and feel great about ourselves when we study. The way you think about tests will help determine how you do in a test-taking situation. Most importantly, how you feel about tests is related to your level of anxiety about test taking. Students who have negative thoughts and feelings about tests become anxious. Students who think positively are less anxious. To reduce test anxiety, try thinking about tests and testing situations using a positive frame of mind.

- **All or Nothing Thinking.**
Nothing is ever as simple as it seems! Sometimes we convince ourselves something is going to be "awful" or "wonderful." Rarely does it turn out that way.

Trouble comes along when students think tests are going to be an "awful" experience. If you dread something happening, it is only going to make things worse. Also, you may be wrong! Nothing is as terrible as it seems. All the negative thoughts you have about the upcoming test cannot possibly be true. Thinking something is "awful" or "terrible" and nothing else only leads to trouble and failure. The more negative you feel about something, the worse things turn out.

Very few things are "all good" or "all bad." This is especially true for tests. Recognizing the "bad" parts of tests can help you be successful. For example, the fact that you need to study for tests, to pay attention while you are taking tests, and to understand there are probably many more fun things to do in school than take tests are all "true" thoughts. "Good" thoughts are just as true, including the good feelings one gets from studying and the chance that you might do well. Having "all or nothing" thinking is going to get you nowhere. Successful and happy students know some experiences are better than others, but they try to look at a situation from all sides.

- **Mind Reading.**
  Some students believe they can read the minds of their parents and teachers. They assume if they do poorly on the Reading OAT, everyone will think they are "dumb" or "lazy." The more their minds create all the terrible things that people may say about them, the more anxious they get. This just increases anxiety and definitely does not help students do well on tests.

- **Catastrophizing.**
  When people catastrophize, they make everything a catastrophe! A catastrophe is a disaster. It is when something terrible happens. When a student catastrophizes, his or her mind goes on and on creating terrible scenes of disasters. If someone put all these ideas into a movie script, the writer might be rich!

  The Reading OAT is an important part of a sixth-grader's school year. It is a test that helps the student, the teacher, and the school. However, a sixth-grade student is much more than just his or her score on the Reading OAT! Each student is an individual who has his or her own great personality, talents, and other successes in school. If what people catastrophized about was really true, the whole world would be a terrible mess! Imagine if your mother cooked a dinner that didn't turn out quite right. This might mean everyone has to go out for fast food, but you wouldn't love your mother any less. It would be catastrophizing if your mother said, "Now that I burned the dinner, none of my kids will love me. They will probably just want to move out as quickly as they can, and my life will be ruined." Catastrophizing about the Reading OAT is just as bad. Thinking that this test is going to be the worst experience of your life and that your future will be ruined will not help you feel comfortable when preparing for and taking the test.

- **Making "Should" Statements.**
  Students make themselves anxious when they think they "should" do everything! They feel they "should" be as smart as everyone else, "should" study more, and "should" not feel anxious about tests. All these thoughts are pretty ridiculous! You can't always be as smart as the next person, and you do not have to study until you drop to do well on tests. Instead of kicking yourself for not being perfect, it is better to think about all the good things you have done in your life. This will help you do better on tests and be happier in your life by reducing your anxiety.

How Do I Replace Worried Thoughts with Positive Ones?

As we have learned, there are all kinds of thoughts that make us anxious, such as feeling we "should" do everything, thinking we can read peoples' minds, catastrophizing, and thinking only bad thoughts about a situation. Learning how to stop these types of thoughts is very important. Understanding your thoughts and doing something about them help control test anxiety.

People who are worried or anxious can become happier when thinking positive thoughts. Even when situations are scary, such as a visit to the dentist, "positive imagery" is helpful. "Positive imagery" means thinking good thoughts to keep from thinking anxious thoughts. Positive and negative thoughts do not go together! If you are thinking something positive, it is almost impossible to think of something negative. Keep this in mind when test anxiety starts to become a bother.

Try these ideas the next time you find yourself becoming anxious.

- **Thoughts of Success.**
  Thinking "I can do it" thoughts can chase away thoughts of failure. Imagine times you were successful, such as when you performed well in a dance recital or figured out a complicated brain teaser. These are good things to think about. Telling yourself you have been successful in the past and can be successful in the future will chase away thoughts of anxiety.

- **Relaxing Thoughts.**
  Some people find that thinking calming or relaxing thoughts is helpful. Picturing a time in which you felt comfortable and happy can lessen your anxious feelings. Imagine yourself playing a baseball game, running through a park, or eating an ice cream cone; these are all positive thoughts that may get in the way of anxious ones. Some students find that listening to music on the morning of a test is helpful. It probably doesn't matter what music you listen to, as long as it makes you feel good about yourself, confident, and relaxed.

  Just as you can calm your mind, it is also important for you to relax your body. Practice relaxing your body. When students have test anxiety, their muscles become stiff. In fact, the whole body becomes tense. Taking deep breaths before a test and letting them out slowly as well as relaxing muscles in your body are all very helpful ways to feel less anxious. Your school counselors will probably have more ideas about relaxation. You may find that relaxation doesn't just help you on tests, but is helpful for other challenging situations and for feeling healthy overall.

- **Don't Let Yourself Feel Alone.**
  Everyone feels more anxious when they feel alone and separate from others. Talking to your friends, parents, and teachers about your feelings helps. Feeling anxious about tests does not mean there is something wrong with you! You will be surprised to find that many of your friends and fellow students also feel anxious about tests. You may be even more surprised to learn your parents and teachers have also had test anxiety. They know what you are going through and are there to support you.

- **Take Care of Yourself!**
  Everyone is busy. Many sixth graders are involved in all sorts of activities, including sports, music, and helping around the house. Often, you are so busy you forget to eat breakfast or you don't get enough sleep. Eating and sleeping right are important, especially before a test like the Reading OAT. If you are not a big breakfast eater, try to find something that you like to eat and get in the habit of eating breakfast. When you do not eat right, you may feel shaky and have a hard time concentrating, and your anxiety can increase. Being tired does not help either. Try to get in the habit of going to bed at a good time every night (especially the night before a test) so you can feel fresh, rested, and confident for the Reading OAT.

- **Practice Your Test-Taking Success.**
  People who have accomplished incredibly difficult goals have used their imaginations to help them achieve success. They thought about what they would do step by step to be successful.

  You can do the same! Think about yourself on the morning of the test. Imagine telling yourself positive thoughts and eating a good breakfast. Think about arriving at school and feeling confident that you will do fine on the test. Imagine closing your eyes before the test, breathing deeply, relaxing, and remembering all the study skills you have learned. The more you program your mind to think in a successful and positive way, the better off you will be.

- **Learn to Use Study Skills.**
  The next chapter in this book will help you learn test-taking strategies. The more you know about taking tests successfully, the calmer you will feel. Knowledge is power! Practice test-taking strategies to reduce your test anxiety.

- **Congratulate Yourself During the Test.**
  Instead of thinking, "I've only done five problems and I've got eight pages to go," or "I knew three answers right, but one mixed me up," reward yourself for what you have done. Tell yourself, "I got some answers right so far, so I bet I can do more." After all, if you don't compliment yourself, who will?

Conclusion

You are not alone if you feel stressed about tests. It is probably good to feel a little anxious, because it motivates you to do well. However, if you feel very anxious about tests, then reading, re-reading, and practicing the suggestions in this chapter will help you "tackle your test anxiety."

Test-Taking Strategies

All Students Can Do Their Best on Tests

Most students want to do their best on tests. Tests are one important way for teachers to know how well students are doing and for students to understand how much progress they are making in their studies. Tests like the Reading OAT help schools measure how well students are learning so teachers and principals can make their schools even better. Students can do the best job possible in "showing what they know" by learning how to be good test takers.

It's just not possible to do a good job without the right tools. Test-taking strategies are tools to help you perform well on tests. Everyone needs good tools and strategies when facing a problem. If you do not have these, even the smartest or most talented person will do poorly. Think about people who are wizards at fixing cars and trucks. Your family's car dies in the middle of the road. The situation looks pretty hopeless. How are you ever going to get to that basketball game tomorrow if your parent's car is a mechanical mess? Suddenly, magic happens! The mechanic at the repair shop calls your parents and tells them the car is ready, just a day after it broke down. How did this happen? It happened because the auto-repair mechanic had a great deal of knowledge about cars. Most importantly, he had the right tools and strategies to fix the car. He knew how to look at the problem, and when he figured out what to do, he had some special tools to get the job done. You can also find special ways that will help you be a successful test taker.

Tools You Can Use on the Reading OAT and Tests Throughout Your Life!

Be An "Active Learner."

You can't learn anything by being a "sponge." Just because you are sitting in a pool of learning (your classroom) does not mean you are going to learn anything just by being there. Instead, students learn when they actively think and participate during the school day. Students who are active learners pay attention to what is being said. They also constantly ask themselves and their teachers questions about the subject. When able, they participate by making comments and joining discussions. Active learners enjoy school, learn more, feel good about themselves, and usually do better on tests. Remember the auto-repair mechanic? That person had a lot of knowledge about fixing cars. All the tools and strategies in the world will not help unless you have benefited from what your teachers have tried to share.

Being an active learner takes time and practice. If you are the type of student who is easily bored or frustrated, it is going to take some practice to use your classroom time differently. Ask yourself the following questions.

- Am I looking at the teachers?
- Do I pay attention to what is being said?
- Do I have any questions or ideas about what the teacher is saying?
- Do I listen to what my fellow students are saying and think about their ideas?
- Do I look at the clock and wonder what time school will be over, or do I appreciate what is happening during the school day and how much I can learn?
- Do I try to think about how my schoolwork might be helpful to me now or in the future?

Although you do need special tools and strategies to do well on tests, the more you learn, the better chance you have of doing well on tests. Think about Kristen!

There was a young girl named Kristen,
Who was bored and wouldn't listen.
She didn't train
To use her smart brain
And never knew what she was missing!

Don't Depend on Luck!
Preparing for the Reading OAT might feel stressful or boring at times, but it is an important part of learning how to show what you know and doing your best. Even the smartest student needs to spend time taking practice tests and listening to the advice of teachers about how to do well. Luck alone is not going to help you do well on the Reading OAT or other tests. People who depend on luck do not take responsibility for themselves. Some people who believe in luck do not want to take the time and effort to do well. It is easier for them to say, "It's not my fault I did poorly. It's just not my lucky day." Some people just do not feel very good about their abilities. They get in the habit of saying, "Whatever happens will happen." They believe they can never do well no matter how much they practice or prepare. Students who feel they have no control over what happens to them usually have poor grades and do not feel very good about themselves.

Your performance on the Reading OAT (and other tests) is not going to be controlled by luck. Instead, you can have a lot of control over how well you do in many areas of your life, including test taking. Don't be like Chuck!

> There was a cool boy named Chuck,
> Who thought taking tests was just luck.
> He never prepared.
> He said, "I'm not scared."
> When his test score appears, he should duck!

Do Your Best Every Day!
Many students find sixth grade much different than other grades. Suddenly, the work seems really hard! Not only that, but your teachers are no longer treating you like a baby. That's good in some ways, because it gives you more freedom and responsibility, but there sure is a lot to learn! You might feel the same way about the Reading OAT; you may feel you'll never be prepared. Many times when we are faced with new challenges, it is easy to just give up.

Students are surprised when they find that if they just set small goals for themselves, they can learn an amazing amount! If you learn just one new fact every day of the year, at the end of the year, you will know 365 new facts. You could use those to impress your friends and family! Now think about what would happen if you learned three new facts every day. At the end of the year, you would have learned 1,095 new facts! Soon you will be on your way to having a mind like an encyclopedia.

When you think about the Reading OAT or any other academic challenge, try to focus on what you can learn step by step and day by day. You will be surprised how all of this learning adds up to make you one of the smartest sixth graders ever! Think about Ray!

> There was a smart boy named Ray,
> Who learned something new every day.
> He was pretty impressed
> With what his mind could possess.
> His excellent scores were his pay!

Get to Know the Reading OAT!
Most sixth graders are probably pretty used to riding in their parents' cars. They know how to make the air-conditioning cooler or warmer, how to change the radio stations, and how to adjust the volume on the radio. Think about being a passenger in a totally unfamiliar car. You might think, "What are all those buttons? How do I even turn on the air conditioner? How do I make the window go up and down?" Now, think about taking the Reading OAT. The Reading OAT is a test, but it may be different than some tests you have taken in the past. The more familiar you are with the types of questions on the Reading OAT and how to record your answers, the better you will do. Working through the Reading Tutorial and Practice Test chapters in this book will help you get to know the Reading OAT. Becoming familiar with the Reading OAT is a great test-taking tool. Think about Sue!

> There was a kid named Sue,
> Who thought her test looked new.
> "I never saw this before!
> How'd I get a bad score?"
> If she practiced, she might have a clue!

Read Directions and Questions Carefully!

One of the worst mistakes a student can make on the Reading OAT is to ignore directions or to read questions carelessly. By the time some students are in the sixth grade, they think they have heard every direction or question ever invented, and it is easy for them to "tune out" directions. Telling yourself, "These directions are just like other directions," or "I'm not really going to take time to read this question because I know what the question will be," are not good test-taking strategies. It is impossible to do well on the Reading OAT without knowing what is being asked.

Reading directions and questions slowly, repeating them to yourself, and asking yourself if what you are reading makes sense are powerful test-taking strategies. Think about Fred!

There was a nice boy named Fred,
Who forgot almost all that he read.
The directions were easy,
But he said, "I don't need these."
He should have read them instead.

Know How to Fill in Those Answer Bubbles!

Most sixth graders have taken tests that ask them to fill in answer bubbles. You might be a very bright sixth grader, but you will never "show what you know" unless you fill in the answer bubbles correctly. Don't forget: a computer will be "reading" your multiple-choice question answers. If you do not fill in the answer bubble darkly or if you use a check mark or dot instead of filling in the bubble completely, your smart thinking will not be counted! Look at the examples given below.

● **Correct**

✗ **Incorrect**

Practice filling in the answer circles here.

○ ○ ○ ○ ○

Learning how to fill in answer bubbles takes practice, practice, and more practice! It may not be how you are used to answering multiple-choice questions, but it is the only way to give a right answer on the Reading OAT. Think about Kay!

> A stubborn girl named Kay
> Liked to answer in her own way.
> Her marked answer bubbles
> Gave her all sorts of troubles.
> Her test scores ruined her day!

Speeding Through the Test Doesn't Help!
Most students have more than enough time to read all of the passages and answer all the questions on the Reading OAT. There will always be some students who finish the test more quickly than others, but this does not mean the test was easier for them or their answers are correct. Whether you finish at a faster rate or at a slower rate than other students in your class is not important. As long as you take your time, are well prepared, concentrate on the test, and use some of the skills in this book, you should be able to do just fine. You will not get a better score just because you finish the test before everyone else. Speeding through a test item or through the whole Reading OAT does not help you do well. In fact, students do their best when they work at a medium rate of speed, not too slow and not too fast. Students who work too slowly tend to get worried about their answers and sometimes change correct answers into incorrect ones. Students who work too fast often make careless mistakes, and many of them do not read directions or questions carefully. Think about Liz.

> There was a sixth grader named Liz,
> Who sped through her test like a whiz.
> She thought she should race
> At a very fast pace,
> But it caused her to mess up her quiz.

Answer Every Question!
There is no reason that you should not attempt to answer every question you encounter on the Reading OAT. Even if you don't know the answer, there are ways for you to increase your chances of choosing the correct response. Use the helpful strategies described below to help you answer every question to the best of your ability.

- **If you don't know the answer, guess!**
  Did you know that on the Reading OAT there is no penalty for guessing? That is really good news! That means you have a one out of four chance of getting a multiple-choice question right, even if you just close your eyes and guess! That means that for every four questions you guess, you should get about 25% (1 out of 4) of the questions right. Guessing alone is not going to make you a star on the Reading OAT, but leaving multiple-choice items blank is not going to help you either.

  Now comes the exciting part! If you can rule out one of the four answer choices, your chances of answering correctly are now one out of three. You can almost see your Reading OAT score improving right before your eyes!

  Although it is always better to be prepared for the test and to study in school, we all have to guess at one time or another. Some of us do not like to guess because we are afraid of choosing the wrong answer, but on the Reading OAT, guessing is better than leaving a question unanswered.

> There was a smart girl named Jess,
> Who thought it was useless to guess.
> If a question was tough,
> She just gave up.
> This only added to her stress.

- **Use a "code" to help you make good guesses on the Reading OAT.**
  Some students use a "code" to rate each answer when they feel they might have to guess. Using your pencil in the test booklet, you can mark the following codes next to each multiple-choice response so you can make the best possible guess. The codes are as follows:

  (+) Putting a "plus sign" by your answer means you are not sure if this answer is correct, but you think this answer is probably more correct than the others.
  (?) Putting a "question mark" by your answer means you are unsure if this is the correct answer, but you don't want to rule it out completely.
  (−) Putting a "minus sign" by your answer means you are pretty sure this is the wrong answer. You should then choose from the other answers to make an educated guess.

Remember, it is fine to write in your test booklet. Think about Dwight!

> There was a smart kid named Dwight,
> Who marked answers that looked to be right.
> He'd put a plus sign
> Or a dash or a line.
> Now the whole world knows he is bright!

- **Use what you know to "power guess."**
Not everything you know was learned in a classroom. Part of what you know comes from just living your life. When you take the Reading OAT, you should use everything you have learned in school, but you should also use your experiences outside the classroom to help you answer questions correctly. Using your "common sense," as well as other information you know, will help you do especially well on the Reading OAT. Try to use what you know from the world around you to eliminate obviously wrong answers. If you can rule out just one answer that you are certain is not correct, you are going to greatly increase your chances of guessing another answer correctly. For example, Think about Drew!

> There was a boy named Drew,
> Who forgot to use what he knew.
> He had lots of knowledge.
> He could have been in college!
> But his right answers were few.

- **Do Not Get Stuck on One Question!**
One of the worst things you can do on the Reading OAT is to get stuck on one question. The Reading OAT gives you many chances to show all that you have learned. Not knowing the answer to one or two questions is not going to hurt your test results very much.

When you become stuck on a question, your mind plays tricks on you. You begin to think that you are a total failure, and your worries become greater and greater. This worrying gets in the way of your doing well on the rest of the test. Remember, very few students know all the answers on the Reading OAT. If you are not sure of the answer after spending some time on it, mark it in your test booklet and come back to it later. When you do come back to that question later, you might find a new way of thinking. Sometimes, another question or answer later in the test will remind you of a possible answer to the question that had seemed difficult. If not, you can use your guessing strategies to solve the questions you are unsure of after you have answered all the questions you know. Also, when you move on from a troubling question and find you are able to answer other questions correctly, you will feel much better about yourself and you will feel calmer. This will help you have a better chance of succeeding on a question that made you feel "stuck." Think about Von.

> There was a sweet girl named Von,
> Who got stuck and just couldn't go on.
> She'd sit there and stare,
> But the answer wasn't there.
> Before she knew it, all the time was gone.

- **Always, and This Means Always, Recheck Your Work!**
Everyone makes mistakes. People make the most mistakes when they feel a little worried or rushed. Checking your work is a very important part of doing your best on the Reading OAT. You can read a paragraph over again if there is something you do not understand or something that you forgot. If an answer does not seem to make sense, go back and reread the question. Think about Cath and Jen!

> A smart young lady named Cath
> Always forgot to recheck her math.
> When she was done,
> She wrote eleven, not one!
> When her test score comes, she won't laugh.

> There was a quick girl named Jen,
> Who read stuff once and never again.
> It would have been nice
> If she'd reread it twice.
> Her test scores would be better then!

- **Pay Attention to Yourself and Not Others.**
It is easy to look around the room and wonder how friends are doing on the Reading OAT. However, it is important to think about how you are using tools and strategies on the Reading OAT. Don't become distracted by friends. You are going to waste a lot of time if you try to figure out what your friends are doing. Instead, use that time to "show what you know."

If it becomes hard for you to pay attention, give yourself a little break. If you feel you are getting a little tense or worried, or if a question seems tough, close your eyes for a second or two. Think positive thoughts about the Reading OAT. Try to put negative thoughts out of your mind. You might want to stretch your arms or feet or move around a little to help you focus. Anything you may do to help pay better attention to the test is a great test-taking strategy. Think about Kirk!

> There was a boy named Kirk,
> Who thought of everything but his work.
> He stared into the air
> And squirmed in his chair.
> When his test scores come, he won't look!

Understanding the OAT for Grade 6 Reading

Introduction

In the Reading section of the Grade 6 OAT, you will be asked questions to test what you have learned so far in school. These questions are based on the reading skills you have been taught in school through sixth grade. The questions you will answer are not meant to confuse or trick you, but are written so you have the best chance to show what you know.

This chapter contains a sample reading passage, followed by sample multiple-choice, short-answer, and extended-response questions. It also contains an Item Distribution chart and scoring information, which show you what type of questions you will see on the Grade 6 Reading OAT. Finally, the chapter provides additional information about the Reading OAT as well as an explanation on how to use the Reading Tutorial chapter.

Questions I Will Answer on the OAT

You will answer multiple-choice, short-answer, and extended-response questions on the Reading OAT. Multiple-choice items have four answer choices, and only one is correct. Short-answer items will require you to write a word, a phrase, or a sentence or two. Extended-response items will require you to write a few phrases, or a complete sentence or short paragraph.

The questions are based on reading selections. The selections may be literary or expository. Literary selections are fiction. Expository selections are informative.

Examples of a literary selection, a multiple-choice item, a short-answer item, an extended-response item, and an Answer Document are shown below and on the next two pages. For multiple-choice questions, you will mark your answer in the answer bubbles in the Answer Document. For short-answer and extended-response questions, you will write your answer in the space provided in the Answer Document. The Reading Tutorial and Practice Tests have sample Answer Documents for you to use to help you become familiar with them.

Stormy Nights

1   Hendrik still felt afraid of storms at night. If he awoke during a thunderstorm, fear seemed to take a grip on his throat until he could barely breathe.

2   Hendrik's bedroom looked ghostly when a storm shook the neighborhood. The room suddenly appeared white during flashes of lightning and then instantly grew darker-than-night during crashes of thunder. The flashes consisted of an unearthly light that shone in fits and starts: it turned on, then off, then on again. It made the room appear to move.

3   Imagine a bedroom rocking like a ship at sea! Hendrik would lie perfectly still under his warm, neat sheets, yet he felt as though he was drowning.

4   By the middle of June, there seemed to be a fresh storm every few nights. Often, the rain fell after midnight. By morning, things would look beautiful and damp. At dawn, the June grass lay like a smooth, green carpet glistening across the world. He tried to picture this at night, but the grass seemed different in darkness. After sunset, nothing looked green or smooth.

5   On the last night in June, Hendrik made himself comfortable on the old porch swing. He sat for a while. The night was completely dark, and it was impossible to see the dark grass. Silently, Hendrik watched and listened. He could hear life in the grass: thousands of crickets were communicating in the night. He thought about these little creatures that spend their entire lives outdoors, drinking the rainwater and the dew they discover on blades of grass. "It's amazing how those tiny insects survive all these turbulent storms," he thought. The sound of their chirping washed around him like gentle waves. The sound was comforting.

Grade 6 Reading

1. What problem does Hendrik face?

   A. The noise made by insects keeps him up at night.

   B. He is scared of thunderstorms.

   C. Hendrik doesn't like living on a ship.

   D. The rain is so loud, he cannot sleep.

2. What caused the room to appear light and then dark? Write your answer in the **Answer Document**. (2 points)

3. Write a sentence describing what Hendrik's bedroom looks like during a thunderstorm. Give at least three examples to describe the room. Write your answer in the **Answer Document**. (4 points)

Sample Answer Document Show What You Know® on the OAT
Grade 6 Reading

1. Ⓐ Ⓑ Ⓒ Ⓓ

   The correct answer is B. You should fill in circle B completely.

2. Write your response to question 2 in the space below.

   _____
   _____
   _____
   _____
   _____
   _____
   _____
   _____
   _____
   _____
   _____
   _____
   _____
   _____

   Hendrik awoke during the night. His bedroom looked light during the flashes of lightning, then grew dark after each flash of lightning.

3. Write your response to question 3 in the space below.

Hendrik's bedroom looks ghostly, looks white during lightning flashes, the room appears to move, and then the room grows darker.

Item Distribution on the OAT for Grade 6 Reading

Number of Items	37
Number of Multiple-Choice Questions	29
Number of Short-Answer Questions	6
Number of Extended-Response Questions	2
Types of Passages	2–3 Informational Texts 2–3 Literary Texts
Length of Passages	2 short (up to 350 words) 2 medium (351–650 words) 1 long (651–900 words)

Note: This is the Item Distribution that will be used on the actual OAT for Grade 6 Reading. Each practice test in this book contains 40 questions.

Scoring

The Reading questions are based on five reading selections. The selections may be literary or expository. Literary selections are fictional. Expository selections are informative.

You will answer multiple-choice, short-answer, and extended-response questions in the Reading OAT. Multiple-choice items have four answer choices, and only one is correct. Short-answer items will require you to write a word, a phrase, or a sentence or two. Extended-response items will require you to write a few phrases, or a complete sentence or short paragraph.

Multiple-Choice Items

Multiple-choice items are used whenever a single, concise answer to the item is possible. The multiple-choice questions on the OAT for Grade 6 Reading emphasize critical thinking over factual recollection. The multiple-choice items are worth one point each. There is no penalty for guessing; an item with no response will be automatically counted as incorrect.

Short-Answer and Extended-Response Items

Conventions of writing (sentence structure, word choice, usage, grammar, spelling, and mechanics) will not affect the scoring of short-answer and extended-response items unless there is interference with the clear communication of ideas.

Short-Answer Scoring

Short-answer items are scored on a 2-point scale. Here is a sample of a 2-point rubric:

A **2-point** response is complete and appropriate. It demonstrates a thorough understanding of the reading selection. It indicates logical reasoning and conclusions. It is accurate, relevant, comprehensive, and detailed.

A **1-point** response is partially appropriate. It contains minor flaws in reasoning or neglects to address some aspect of the item or question. It is mostly accurate and relevant but lacks comprehensiveness. It demonstrates an incomplete understanding of the reading selection or inability to make coherent meaning from the text.

A **Zero** is assigned if there is no response or if the response indicates no understanding of the reading selection or item.

A **NS (Non-Scorable)** is assigned if the response is unreadable, illegible, or written in a language other than English.

Extended-Response Scoring

Extended-response items will be scored on a 4-point scale. Here is a sample of a 4-point rubric:

A **4-point** response provides extensive evidence of the kind of interpretation called for in the item or question. The response is well-organized, elaborate, and thorough. It demonstrates a complete understanding of the whole work as well as how parts blend to form the whole. It is relevant, comprehensive, and detailed, demonstrating a thorough understanding of the reading selection. It thoroughly addresses the important elements of the question. It contains logical reasoning and communicates effectively and clearly.

A **3-point** response provides evidence that an essential interpretation has been made. It is thoughtful and reasonably accurate. It indicates an understanding of the concept or item, communicates adequately, and generally reaches reasonable conclusions. It contains some combination of the following flaws: minor flaws in reasoning or interpretation, failure to address some aspect of the item, or the omission of some detail.

A **2-point** response is mostly accurate and relevant. It contains some combination of the following flaws: incomplete evidence of interpretation, unsubstantial statements made about the text, an incomplete understanding of the concept or item, lack of comprehensiveness, faulty reasoning, and/or unclear communication.

A **1-point** response provides little evidence of interpretation. It is unorganized and incomplete. It exhibits decoding rather than reading. It demonstrates a partial understanding of the item but is sketchy and unclear. It indicates some effort beyond restating the item. It contains some combination of the following flaws: little understanding of the concept or item, failure to address most aspects of the item, or inability to make coherent meaning from text.

A **Zero** is assigned if the response shows no understanding of the item or if the student fails to respond to the item.

A **NS (Non-Scorable)** is assigned if the response is unreadable, illegible, or written in a language other than English.

Additional Information

- All work should be done in the Student Workbook. All answers should be written in the Answer Document. By doing so, you will become familiar with answering various types of questions within the spaces provided.
- You are not penalized for incorrect answers. It is to your benefit to answer all questions.
- You are **not** permitted to use reference materials, such as print or electronic dictionaries, thesauruses, or spell-check software during the test.

Time Allotment

There is no time limit as you take the Tutorial and Practice Tests in this workbook. You will have two and one-half hours to complete the Reading OAT.

Using the Reading Tutorial

The Reading Tutorial, which begins on page 35, identifies the Content Standards you need to review before taking the actual Reading OAT. The Reading Tutorial contains multiple-choice, short-answer, and extended-response questions. A sample Answer Document is located next to the question to help you become familiar with how to write your answer in the space allowed. An analysis for each question is given to help you identify the correct answer.

Glossary

acronyms: Words or indicators formed from the initial letters of a name, such as OAT for Ohio Achievement Test.

affixes: Groups of syllables (i.e. prefixes, such as anti- or post-, and suffixes, such as -ly or -ment) which, when added to a word or a root, alters the meaning of the word.

alliteration: The repetition of the same sound, usually of a consonant, at the beginning of two or more words of a sentence or line of poetry (e.g., "Andrew Alligator always eats alphabet soup").

alliterative sentences: Repeating the same initial sound in two or more words of a sentence or line of poetry (e.g., Whitman's line, "all summer in the sound of the sea").

analogy: A comparison of two pairs that have the same relationship. The key is to discover the relationship between the first pair, so you can choose the correct second pair (e.g., part-to-whole, opposites).

analysis: Separation of a whole into its parts for individual study.

analyze: To compare in order to rank items by importance or to provide reasons. Identify the important parts that make up the whole and determine how the parts are related to one another.

anticipation guide: A flexible strategy used to activate students' thoughts and opinions about a topic and to link their prior knowledge to new material. For example, a series of teacher-generated statements about a topic that students respond to and discuss before reading.

antonyms: Words that mean the opposite (e.g., light is an antonym of dark).

assumptions: Statements or thoughts taken to be true without proof.

author's craft: Stylistic choices the author makes regarding such components as plot, characterization, structure, scenes, and dialogue to produce a desired effect.

author's perspective: The author's subjective view as reflected in his/her written expression.

author's purpose: The reason an author writes, such as to entertain, inform, or persuade.

author's style: The author's attitude as reflected in the format of the author's written expression.

author's tone: The author's attitude as reflected in the word choice of the author's written expression.

automaticity: Ability to recognize a word (or series of words) in text effortlessly and rapidly.

blend: In decoding, it is the reader's act of sounding out and then combining the sounds in a word to assist in the pronunciation.

common consonant sounds: Speech sounds made by obstructing air flow, causing audible friction in varying amounts. Common consonant sounds include: /b/, /k/, /d/, /f/, /g/, /h/, /j/, /l/, /m/, /n/, /p/, /kw/, /r/, /s/, /t/, /v/, /w/, /ks/, /y/, /z/.

common inflectional ending: A common suffix that changes the form or function of a word, but not its basic meaning, such as "-ed" in "sprayed," "-ing" in "gathering."

common sight words: Words that are immediately recognized as a whole and do not require word analysis for identification. These words usually have irregular spellings.

common vowel patterns: A vowel is the open sound. The mouth must be open to produce the sound of a vowel in a syllable. The most common vowel patterns are the sound/spellings that students encounter most frequently in text (e.g., ea, ee, oi, ow, ou, oo).

comprehension-monitoring strategies: Strategies used to monitor one's reading by being aware of what one does understand and what one does not understand. The reader's awareness determines which comprehension-repair strategies to apply.

comprehension-repair strategies: Strategies used by a reader to regain comprehension as a result of comprehension monitoring. These strategies include but are not limited to: re-reading, word recognition strategies, looking back, reading ahead, slowing down, paraphrasing by sections, using context, and taking notes. (Also referred to as "fix-up strategies.")

comprehension strategies: A procedure or set of steps to follow in order to enhance text understanding (e.g., making inferences, predicting outcomes).

concepts of print: Insights about the ways in which print works. Basic concepts about print include: identification of a book's front and back covers and title page; directionality (knowledge that readers and writers in English move from left to right, top to bottom, front to back); spacing (distance used to separate words); recognition of letters and words; connection between spoken and written language; understanding of the function of capitalization and punctuation; sequencing and locating skills.

content area vocabulary: Vocabulary found in specific subject areas (e.g., "integer" in math and "pioneer" in social studies).

Glossary

content/academic text: Text from literature, science, social studies, math, and other academic areas that students need to read to be academically successful in school.

context: The social or cultural situation in which the spoken or written word occurs; also often used to refer to the material surrounding an unknown word.

context clues: Information from the surrounding text that helps identify a word or word group. Clues could be words, phrases, sentences, illustrations, syntax, typographic signals, definitions, examples, or restatements.

culturally relevant: Reading materials with which students in a classroom can identify or relate. Depending on the student cultural make-up in a classroom, relevant reading material can change from year to year.

decodable text: Reading materials that provide an intermediate step between words in isolation and authentic literature. Such texts are designed to give students an opportunity to learn to use their understanding of phonics in the course of reading connected text. Although decodable texts may contain sight words that have been previously taught, most words are wholly decodable on the basis of the letter-sound and spelling-sound correspondences taught and practiced in phonics lessons.

directionality: Understanding that materials printed in English progress from left to right and top to bottom.

electronic sources: Resources for gathering information such as the Internet, television, radio, CD-ROM encyclopedia, and so on.

elements of style: Word choice, voice, sentence structure, and sentence length.

environmental print: Any print found in the physical environment, such as street signs, billboards, labels, and business signs.

figurative language: Word images and figures of speech used to enrich language (e.g., simile, metaphor, personification).

fluency: Ability to read a text quickly with accuracy and expression; freedom from word-identification problems that might hinder comprehension in silent reading or the expression of ideas in oral reading; automaticity.

foreshadowing: A literary technique of giving clues about an event before it happens.

functional document: A technical document such as a business letter, computer manual, or trade publication that assists one in getting information in order to perform a task.

generalize: Taking what is known and using it to make an inference about the nature of similar text. Generalizations lead to transferable understandings that can be supported by fact. They describe the characteristics of classes or categories of persons, places, living and non-living things, and events.

genres: Terms used to classify literary and informational works into categories (e.g., biography, mystery, historical fiction).

gist: The most central thought or idea in a text.

graphic features: Features that illustrate information in text such as graphs, charts, maps, diagrams, tables, etc.

graphic organizers: Organizers that provide a visual representation of facts and concepts from a text and their relationships within an organized frame. Valuable instructional tools used to show the order and completeness of a student's thought process graphically.

icons: Symbols on a computer screen that represent a certain function, command, or program on the computer's hard drive. When an icon is clicked on, some action is performed, such as opening or moving a file, making computing more user-friendly.

idiom: A word used in a special way that may be different from the literal meaning (e.g., "you drive me crazy" or "hit the deck").

independent level: The level at which the student reads fluently with excellent comprehension. The student demonstrates 95–100% comprehension of text.

infer: To understand something not directly stated in the text by using past experience and knowledge combined with the text.

inference: The reasoning involved in drawing a conclusion or making a logical judgment on the basis of indirect evidence and prior conclusions rather than direct evidence from the text.

inferred: Reached a specific conclusion using past experiences and knowledge combined with text evidence.

Glossary

inflectional ending: A letter or group of letters which when added to the end of a word does not change its part of speech, but adjusts the word to fit the meaning of the sentence (e.g., girl, girls, jump, jumped, big, bigger).

informational/expository text: A form of written composition that has as its primary purpose explanation or the communication of details, facts, and discipline- or content-specific information (e.g., content area textbooks, encyclopedias, biographies).

instructional level: The level at which the student can make maximum progress in reading with teacher guidance. The student demonstrates 90–94% comprehension of text.

irony: The use of words to convey the opposite of their literal meaning: the words say one thing, but mean another. Often meant to reflect the author's tone or the attitude of a character or situation.

key word searches: A key term or phrase the computer uses in order to begin an online search for specific information.

language registry: The systematic differences of language use determined by regional, social or situational changes (e.g., a child might say "yup" at home, but would be expected to say "yes" at school).

letter patterns: Common letter groupings that represent specific sounds (e.g., "ing" in "string" and "ough" in "enough").

literary devices: Techniques used to convey or enhance an author's message or voice (e.g., idiom, figurative language, metaphor, exaggeration, dialogue, and imagery).

literary/narrative genres: Subcategories used to classify literary works, usually by form, technique, or content (e.g., novel, essay, short story, comedy, epic).

literary/narrative text: Text that describes action or events; usually includes a problem and resolution; usually, but not always, fiction.

main idea: The gist of a passage; central thought; the chief topic of a passage which can be expressed or implied in a word or phrase; the topic sentence of a paragraph; a statement in sentence form which gives the stated or implied major topic of a passage and the specific way in which the passage is limited in content or reference.

mental imagery: Words or phrases that appeal to one or more of the five senses, allowing the reader to form mental pictures or images while reading.

metaphor: A figure of speech that compares two things without using the words like or as (e.g., laughter is the best medicine).

mood: The emotional state of mind expressed by an author or artist in his/her work, or the emotional atmosphere produced by an artistic work.

multiple-meaning words: Words with the same spelling and/or pronunciation which have more than one meaning depending on their context, such as "The wind blew" and "Please wind the clock."

non-technical documents: In this context, non-technical refers to documents (e.g., memos, lists, job applications) in which the content and vocabulary are not tied to a specific subject.

oddity tasks: In phonemic awareness, identifying which word in a set of three or four has the "odd" sound (e.g., run, rug, and toy).

onomatopoeia: A term used to describe words whose pronunciations suggest their meaning (e.g., meow, buzz). Words used to represent a sound.

onset and rime: Parts of spoken language that are syllables. An onset is the initial consonant(s) sound of a syllable (the onset of bag is b-; of swim, sw-). A rime is the part of the syllable that contains the vowel and all that follows it (the rime of bag is -ag; of swim, -im). Not all syllables or words have an onset, but they all have a rime (e.g., the word or syllable "out" is a rime without an onset).

oral language structure: Spoken language has five linguistic systems. They include the phonological (sounds of language), the syntactic (order and grammar), the semantic (meanings), the pragmatic (social interactive), and lexicon (vocabulary).

organizational features: Tools the author uses to organize ideas (e.g., caption and headings).

organizational structures: The organization of a text.

personification: A figure of speech in which nonhuman objects, such as ideas, objects, or animals, are given human characteristics (e.g., "flowers danced about the lawn").

persuasive devices: A technique the author uses to move the reader to his/her point of view, such as bias, overgeneralization, and association.

Glossary

phoneme: The smallest unit of sound in a spoken word that makes a difference in the word's meaning.

phonemic awareness: The ability to hear, identify, and manipulate individual sounds (phonemes) in spoken words.

phonics: The understanding that there is a predictable relationship between phonemes (the sounds of spoken language) and graphemes (the letters and spellings that represent those sounds in written language).

phonological awareness: A general understanding of the sound structure of words, including rhymes, syllables, and phonemes.

plot: The structure of the events in a story, usually including rising action, climax, and resolution.

point of view: The perspective from which a story is told. The three points of view are first person, third person, and omniscient.

predict: To foresee what might happen in a text based on textual clues and a reader's background knowledge or schema.

predictions: Foretelling what might happen next in a story or poem by using textual clues and a reader's background knowledge or schema.

prefix: An affix attached before a base word or root, such as re- in reprint. A prefix slightly alters the meaning of a root word. For example, reprint means to print again.

primary sources: The original source of resource information (e.g., letter, encyclopedia, book).

print conventions: The rules that govern the customary use of print in reading and writing including directionality of print, punctuation, and capitalization.

prior knowledge: The knowledge that stems from previous experience. Note: prior knowledge is a key component of the schema theory of reading comprehension.

propaganda: Written or oral presentations intended to persuade the audience to a particular point of view often by misrepresenting data or exaggerating the facts.

propaganda techniques: Methods used in creating propaganda, such as bandwagon, peer pressure, repetition, and testimonials/endorsements.

pull-down menu: A computer term that refers to a list of words that appears when the cursor is on a menu item. Also called a drop down list box.

questioning strategies: In these strategies a reader asks questions about a text before, during, and after reading and then searches for answers (e.g., Question Answer Response (QAR); Survey, Question, Read, Recite, Review (SQ3R)).

root words: Meaningful base form of a complex word, after all affixes are removed. A root may be independent, or free, as "read" in unreadable, or may be dependent, or bound, as "-liter-" (from the Greek word for letter) in illiterate.

sarcasm: A remark used to "make fun of" or "put down" someone or something. The remark is not sincere and is often intended to hurt someone's feelings.

scan: To examine or read something quickly, but selectively, for a purpose.

scanning: Examining or reading something quickly, but selectively, for a purpose.

schema: The accumulated knowledge drawn from life experiences that a person has to help understand concepts, roles, emotions, and events.

secondary sources: Sources of information that are derived from primary or original sources (e.g., gossip).

segment: The act of separating the sounds in a word in order to assist decoding or spelling.

semantic mapping: A graphic display of a cluster of words that are meaningfully related.

sentence structure: Any of a number of basic sentence types in a language. The pattern or structure of word order in sentences, clauses, or phrases.

sequence: The arrangement or ordering of information, content, or ideas (e.g., chronological, easy to difficult, part to whole).

sequential: Marked by an arrangement or order of information, content, or ideas, such as part to whole, easy to difficult, etc.

setting: The time(s) and place(s) in which a narrative takes place.

short vowel sounds: The sound of /a/ as in cat, /e/ as in hen, /i/ as in fit, /o/ as in hot, and /u/ as in pup.

sight words: Words that are immediately recognized as wholes and do not require word analysis for identification.

Glossary

similes: Figures of speech comparing two unlike things usually using like or as (e.g., Like ancient trees, we die from the top).

skim: To read or glance through quickly.

story elements: The critical parts of a story, including character, setting, plot, problem, solution. At upper grades, the terms problem and solution change to conflict and resolution.

story structure: The pattern of organization in narration that characterizes a particular type of story.

structural analysis: The identification of word-meaning elements, such as re- and read in reread, to help understand the meaning of a word as a whole.

sub-genres: Genres within other genres (e.g., haiku is a sub-genre of poetry, and mystery is a sub-genre of fiction).

subplot: A minor collection of events in a novel or drama that have some connection with the main plot and should (1) comment on, (2) complicate/defeat, or (3) support the main plot.

suffix: An affix attached to the end of a base, root, or stem that changes the meaning or grammatical function of the word (e.g., -en added to ox to form oxen).

summarize: To determine what is important in the text, condense this information, and put it into the students' own words.

summary: A synthesis of the important ideas in a text presented in a condensed form.

syllabication: Division of words into syllables. A syllable is a word part that contains a vowel, or in spoken language a vowel sound (e-vent; news-pa-per; ver-y).

synonym: A word having a meaning similar to that of another word.

task-oriented text: Text written specifically to direct the reader as to how to complete a task.

technical: Content or vocabulary directly related to specific knowledge or information in a career or interest area.

text complexity: Text demands on the reader increase substantially throughout the grades. Items that influence complexity of text include: highly specialized vocabulary and concepts; abstract concepts presented with minimal context; increased concept load/density; readability considerations; and unique writing patterns in informational text.

text features: A prominent characteristic of a particular type of text, such as chapter titles, sub-headings, and bold-faced words in a history text.

text organizational structures: Expository text is structured in certain ways. The five text structures that students are most likely to encounter are cause-effect, compare/contrast, description, problem/solution, and chronological or time order.

theme: A topic; a major idea or proposition broad enough to cover the entire scope of a literary work. Note: a theme may be stated or implicit, but clues to it may be found in the ideas that are given special prominence or tend to recur in a work.

unfamiliar text: Unseen, unpracticed reading material.

vocabulary strategies: A systematic plan to increase understanding of words (e.g., categorizing and classifying, semantic mapping, semantic feature analysis, concept of definition maps, analogies, using the dictionary and other reference materials, using word parts, using morphemic analysis, using context clues).

word families: A collection of words that share common orthographic rimes (e.g., thank, prank, dank).

word recognition strategies: Strategies for determining the pronunciation and meaning of words in print.

Reading Tutorial

Reading R

Directions:

Today you will be taking the Ohio Grade 6 Reading Tutorial. Three different types of questions appear on this test: multiple choice, short answer, and extended response.

There are several important things to remember:

1. Read each question carefully. Think about what is being asked. Look carefully at graphs or diagrams because they help you understand the question.

2. For short-answer and extended-response questions, write your answers neatly and clearly in the space provided in the answer document. Any answers you write in the Student Workbook will not be scored.

3. Short-answer questions are worth two points. Extended-response questions are worth four points. Point values are printed near each question in your Student Workbook. The amount of space provided for your answers is the same for two- and four-point questions.

4. For multiple-choice questions, shade in the circle next to your choice in the answer document for the test question. Mark only one choice for each question. Darken completely the circles on the answer document. If you change an answer, make sure that you erase your old answer completely.

5. Do not spend too much time on one question. Go on to the next question and return to the question skipped after answering the remaining questions.

6. Check over your work when you are finished.

Go to next page

The Joker

1   "What did one pencil say to the other pencil?" Marshall asked the small crowd of students standing in front of him.

2   "What?" they shouted back with glee.

3   "Hey, baby. You're looking sharp!" Marshall answered and the crowd roared with laughter.

4   Marshall reigned as the sixth-grade "class clown." Everyday Marshall would come to school with a new joke or two to share with his schoolmates during their lunch hour.

5   "He's as funny as a roller-skating flamingo!" exclaimed Angelina. "I listen to his jokes every day. He never says the same joke twice. It's unbelievable how funny Marshall is!"

6   The other students agreed with Angelina. Marshall was the most popular boy during the lunch hour. Everyone swarmed like a colony of bees for seats near him. A few students even got his autograph, swearing that Marshall would become a famous comedian in the future.

7   Even though many students would argue that they were Marshall's biggest fans, Marshall knew that his biggest fan was his best friend and next-door neighbor Sam. Sam was very smart—a straight-A student, in fact. But he never got the same recognition as his famous funny friend Marshall.

8   "How do you do it?" Sam asked Marshall one day while on their way to English class. "How do you come up with so many jokes?"

9   "It's a secret, but I guess I will tell you since you are my biggest fan," said Marshall. He looked around the hall then mischievously tiptoed over to the janitorial closet. "Quick, in here!" he told Sam.

10   They quickly ducked into the small janitorial closet and Marshall revealed his secret. "I get my jokes via the world wide web."

11   "No way!" Sam gasped. "And all this time I thought . . ." *Now, this is really something to laugh about*, Sam thought and he let himself chuckle. What a surprise!

12   The next day Marshall announced his joke during the lunch hour as usual, but he gave Sam a wink at the end of it. Sam laughed hysterically. He would never tell the other students his friend's funny little secret.

Question 1 assesses:

Acquisition of Vocabulary Standard

Benchmark A: Use context clues and text structures to determine the meaning of new vocabulary.

1. Define the meaning of unknown words by using context clues and the author's use of definition, restatement and example.

Reading R

1. "He looked around the hall then **mischievously** tiptoed over to the janitorial closet."

   What does the word **mischievously** mean in the sentence above?

   A. gravely

   B. unknowingly

   C. sincerely

   D. naughtily

1. Ⓐ Ⓑ Ⓒ Ⓓ

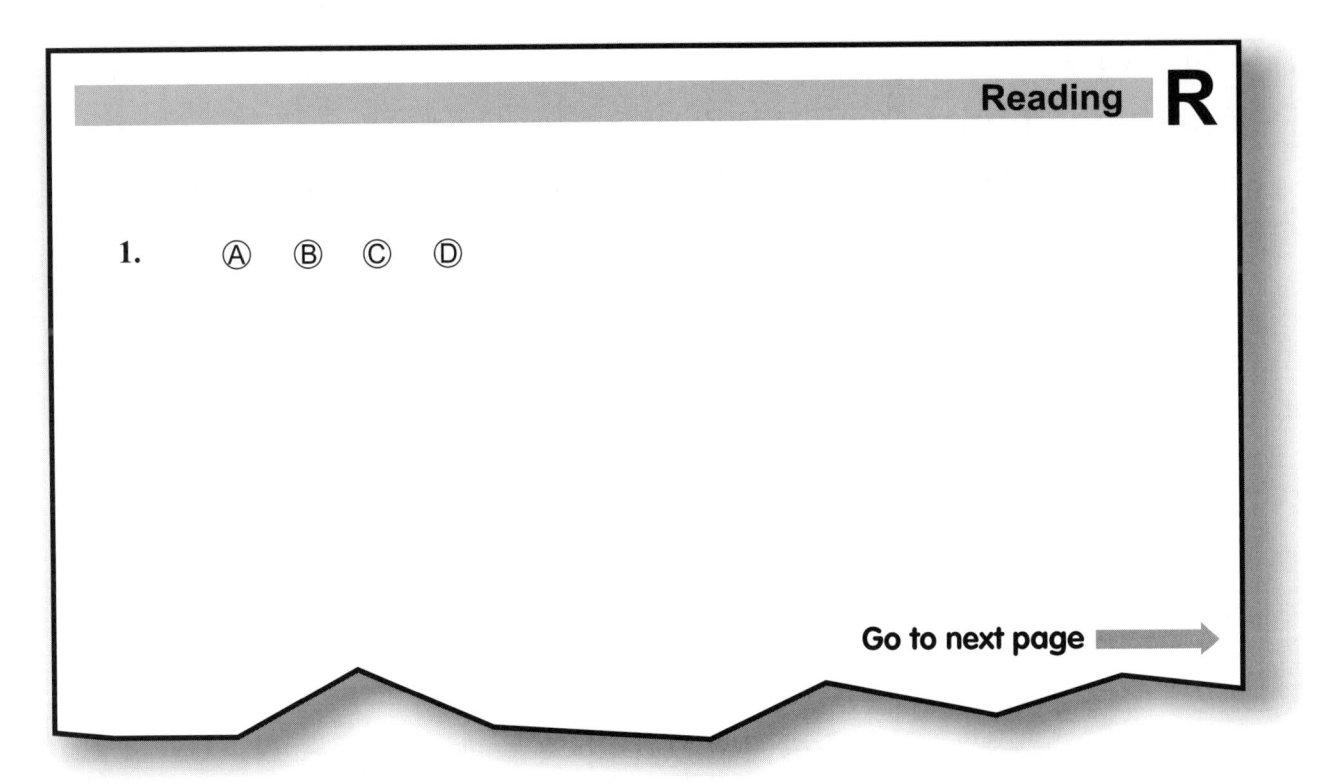

Analysis: *The word mischievously means naughtily. By using context clues in the sentence such as "tiptoed," the reader can come to the conclusion that Marshall and Sam were going somewhere where they should not be—the janitorial closet. Choice D is correct. Choice A is incorrect because gravely means sober and serious, and the boys were neither sober nor serious. Choice B is incorrect. Marshall knows that he is going to tell Sam his secret. Choice C is incorrect. Marshall is not being sincere, he is acting naughtily.*

Question **2** *assesses:*

Acquisition of Vocabulary Standard

Benchmark B: Infer word meaning through identification and analysis of analogies and other word relationships.

3. Identify analogies and other word relationships, including synonyms and antonyms, to determine the meaning of words.

Reading R

2. *"Now, this is really something to **laugh** about,* Sam thought, and he let himself chuckle."

   What is a synonym for the word **laugh** in the sentence above?

   A. cry

   B. chuckle

   C. exclaim

   D. shout

Show What You Know® on the OAT — Tutorial

Grade 6 Reading

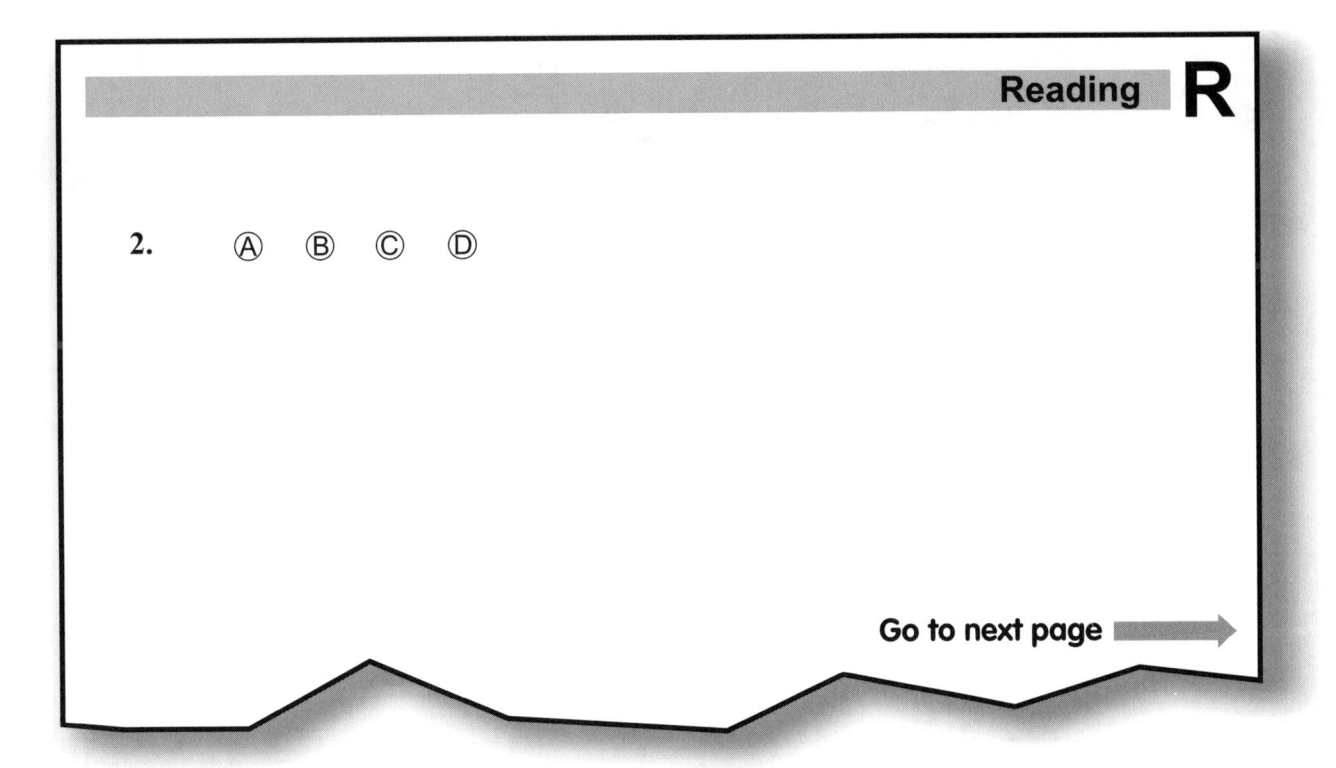

Reading R

2. Ⓐ Ⓑ Ⓒ Ⓓ

Go to next page →

Analysis: *A synonym is a word that has a meaning similar to that of another word. The word chuckle has the same meaning as laugh. Choice B is correct. Choice A is incorrect. Cry is the antonym of the word laugh; it means the opposite of the word laugh. Choices C and D are incorrect. These words do not have the same meaning as the word laugh.*

Question 3 assesses:

Acquisition of Vocabulary Standard

Benchmark B: Infer word meaning through identification and analysis of analogies and other word relationships.

4. Interpret metaphors and similes to understand new uses of words and phrases in text.

Reading R

3. Which sentence from the selection is an example of a simile?

   A. "Marshall was the most popular boy during the lunch hour."

   B. "You're looking sharp!"

   C. "Everyone swarmed like a colony of bees for seats near him."

   D. "I get my jokes via the world wide web."

Go to next page

Grade 6 Reading

Reading R

3. Ⓐ Ⓑ Ⓒ Ⓓ

Go to next page →

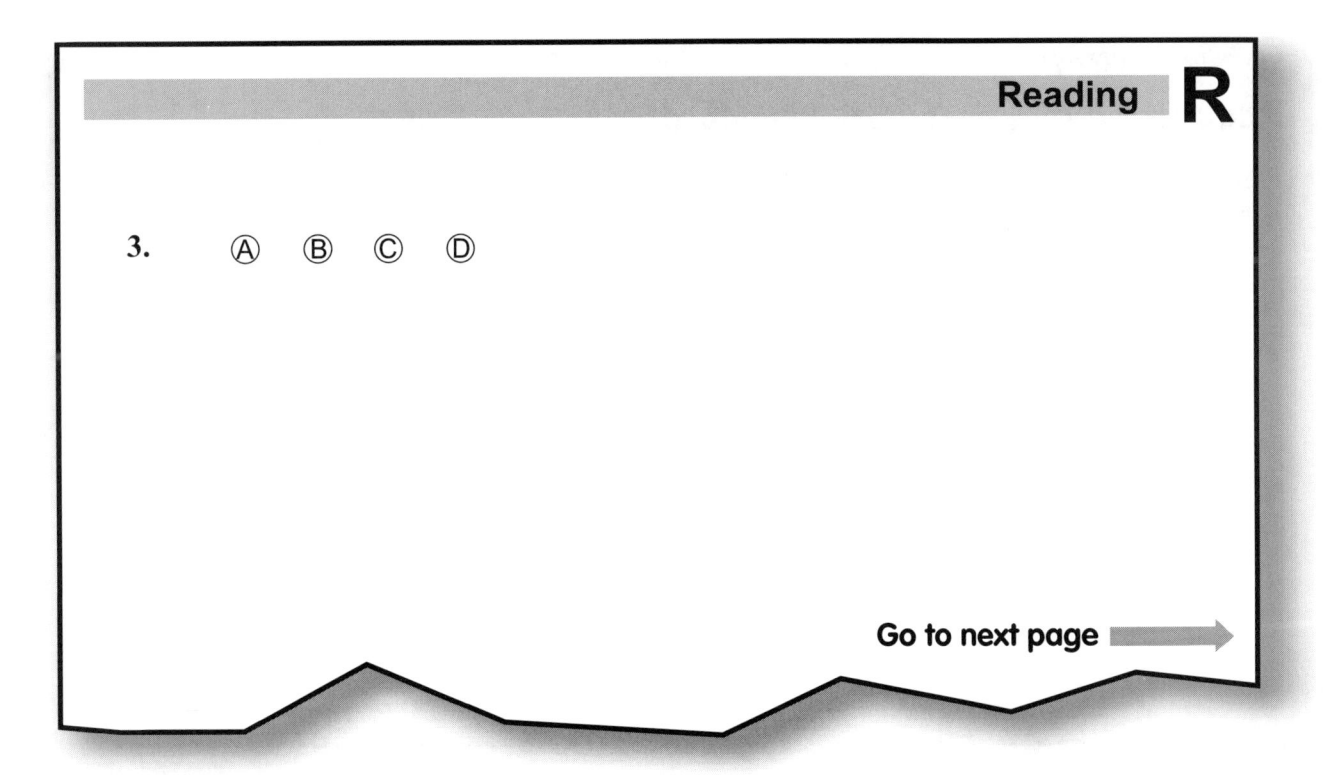

Analysis*: A simile compares two unlike objects using the words like or as. Choice C compares the students to bees using the word like. Choice C is correct. Choices A, B, and D are incorrect. These answers do not compare two unlike objects using the words like or as.*

Question **4** *assesses:*

Acquisition of Vocabulary Standard

Benchmark C: Apply knowledge of connotation and denotation to learn the meanings of words.

2. Apply knowledge of connotation and denotation to determine the meaning of words.

Reading R

4. " 'Hey, baby. You're looking sharp!' Marshall answered and the crowd roared with **laughter**."

   What is the correct meaning of the word **laughter** in the sentence above?

   A. the way a person looks while laughing

   B. the sound or an act of laughing

   C. happy

   D. angry

Go to next page ➡

Show What You Know® on the OAT — Tutorial

Grade 6 Reading

Reading R

4. Ⓐ Ⓑ Ⓒ Ⓓ

Go to next page ➡

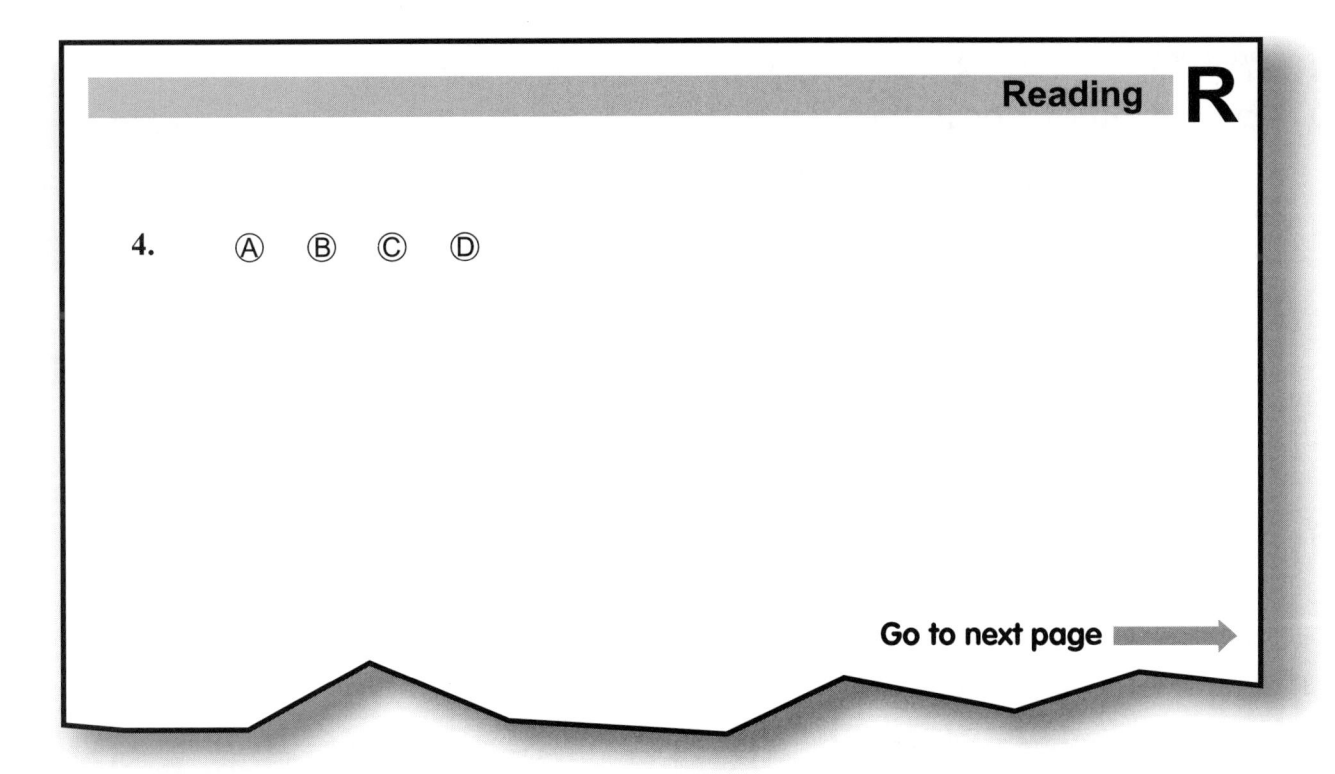

Analysis: This benchmark tests your ability to understand the denotation and connotation of words. Denotation is the definition of the word. Connotation is the feeling associated with the word. The second answer choice is the correct definition of laughter. Choice B is correct. Choice A is incorrect. Laughter is the sound or an act of laughing, not how a person looks while laughing. Choices C and D are incorrect. These answer choices refer to the connotation of the word laughter.

Tutorial

Question 5 assesses:

Acquisition of Vocabulary Standard

Benchmark D: Use knowledge of symbols, acronyms, word origins and derivations to determine the meanings of unknown words.

5. Recognize and use words from other languages that have been adopted in the English language.

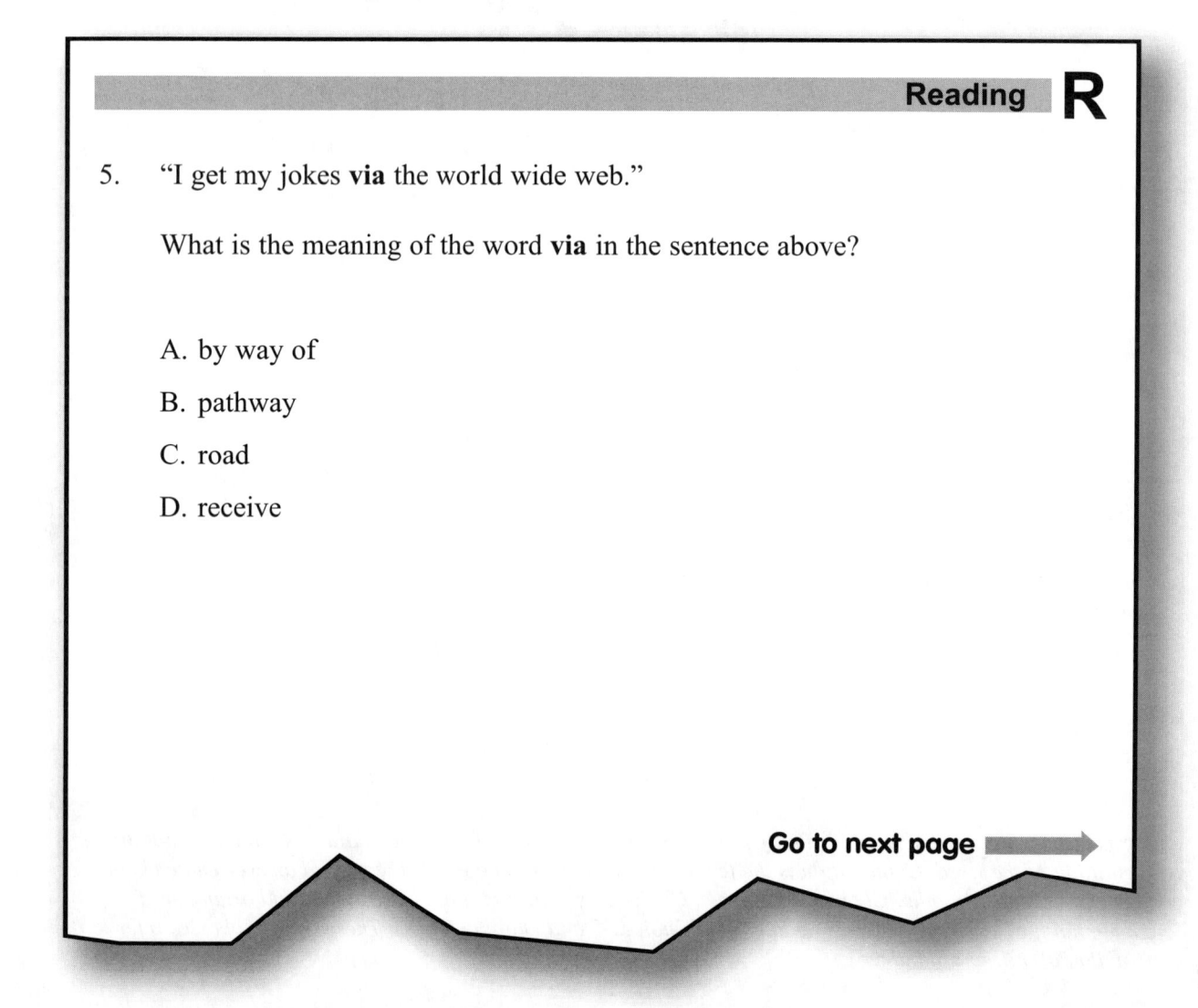

Reading R

5. "I get my jokes **via** the world wide web."

   What is the meaning of the word **via** in the sentence above?

   A. by way of
   B. pathway
   C. road
   D. receive

   Go to next page

5. Ⓐ Ⓑ Ⓒ Ⓓ

Go to next page ➡

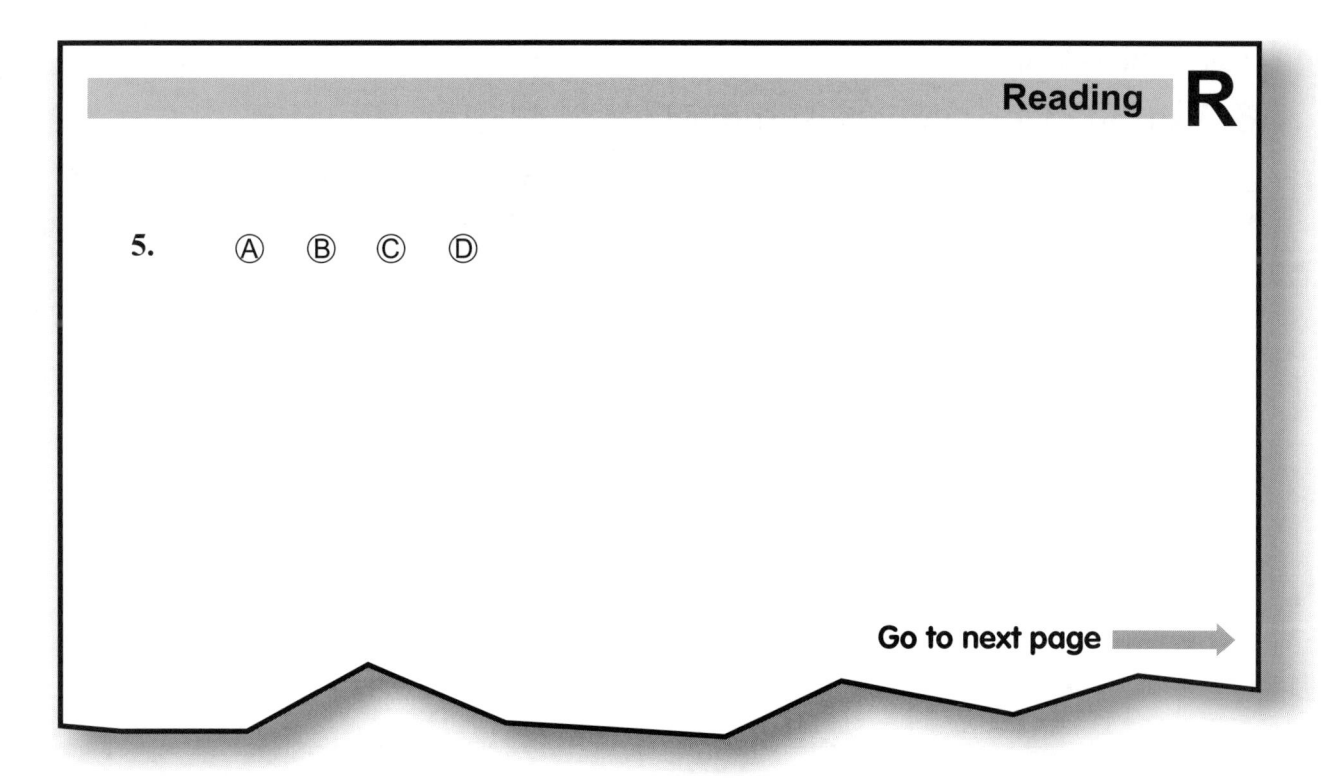

Analysis: *The word via comes from Latin roots and is found in romantic languages, such as French. This word has transcended into the English language. The word via means by way of. This choice correctly uses context clues to identify the correct meaning of the word. Choice A is correct. Choices B and C are incorrect. The words pathway and road are nouns, and via is used as a preposition. Choice D is incorrect. Receive is a verb and via is used as a preposition.*

Tutorial

Question 6 assesses:

Acquisition of Vocabulary Standard

Benchmark D: Use knowledge of symbols, acronyms, word origins and derivations to determine the meanings of unknown words.

7. Identify symbols and acronyms and connect them to whole words.

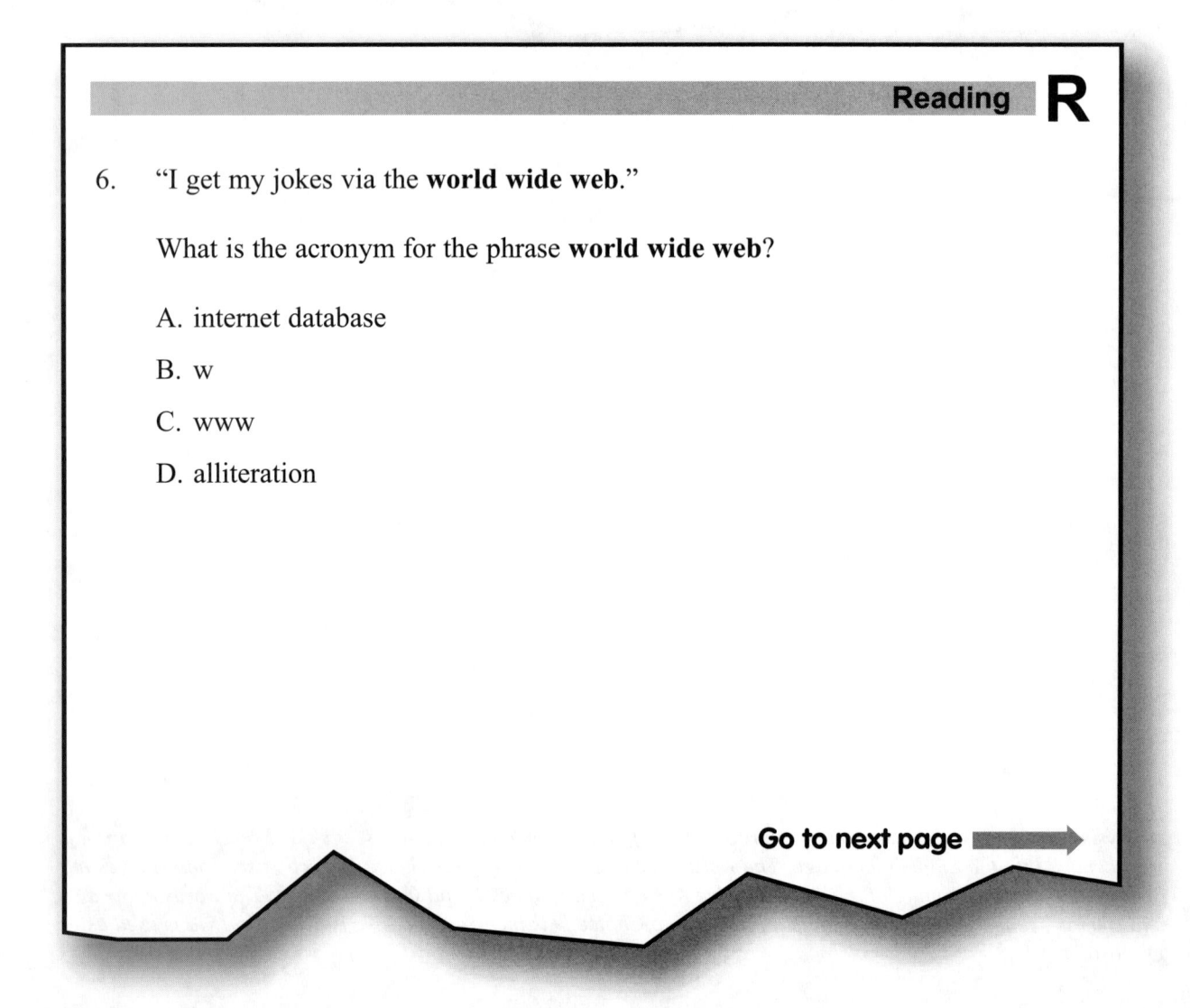

Reading R

6. "I get my jokes via the **world wide web**."

   What is the acronym for the phrase **world wide web**?

   A. internet database

   B. w

   C. www

   D. alliteration

Go to next page ➡

6.   Ⓐ   Ⓑ   Ⓒ   Ⓓ

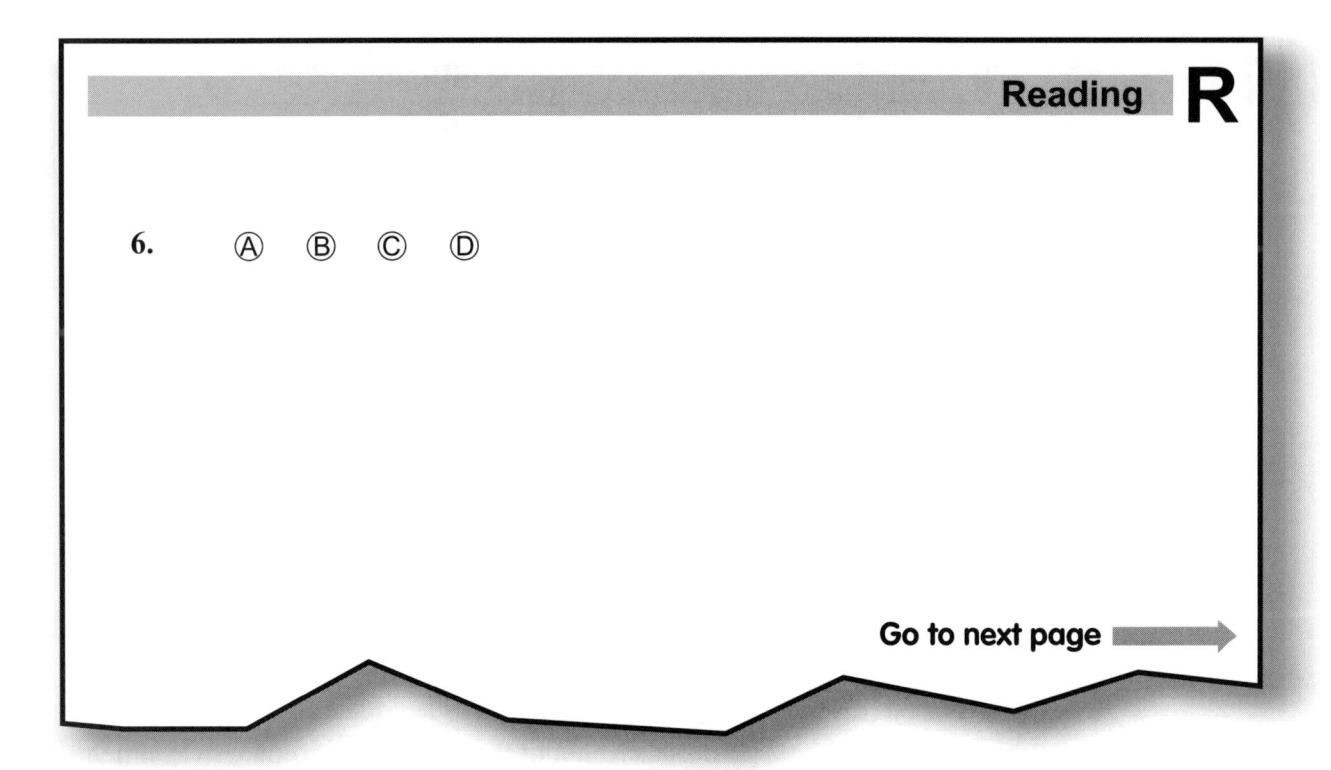

Go to next page

Analysis*: An acronym is a word or an identifier formed from the initials or other parts of several words, such as www is the acronym for world wide web. Choice C is correct. Choice A is incorrecr because this renamed the phrase, but it is not the phrase's acronym. Choice B is incorrect because w is not a complete acronym for world wide web. Choice D is incorrect. The phrase uses alliteration, but this is not the phrase's acronym.*

Reading

A Trip to the Aquarium

1   **Shedd Aquarium, Chicago, Illinois**—*This could possibly be my most favorite place in the world*, I thought as I walked out of Shedd Aquarium with my father and looked back onto its giant white pillars. Thoughts of sea otters, dolphins, sharks, fish, turtles, and my favorite animal, the beluga whale, swam through my head. All I could do was smile and dream of the next time I would come back to the aquarium.

2   When I first arrived at the aquarium, I was very excited. I had always loved underwater creatures and I had recently decided that I would like to become a marine biologist[1] when I grow up. My father surprised me with a trip to the aquarium after I finished a research paper on animals of the Pacific Ocean for school. Going to Shedd Aquarium would let me get a close-up look at the creatures I had learned so much about, but had never seen.

3   First, I visited the Caribbean Coral Reef exhibit. I saw fish, sharks, rays, and the reef. A diver hand-fed the animals in the tank and talked about the creatures and the environment in the Caribbean Coral Reef.

4   I then visited the Fish From Around the World exhibit. Fish from every place you could imagine swam in 80 different tanks. I learned that fish were a very diverse species and that they lived in many different types of environments. Following this my father and I ate lunch at the Bubble Net Food Court and talked about all the creatures we had seen that morning.

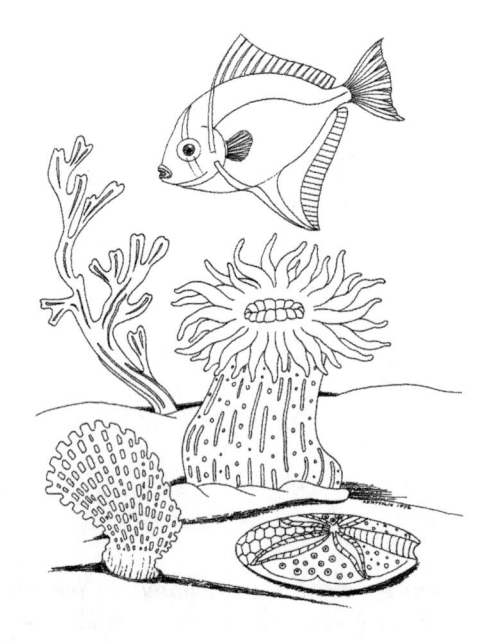

Go to next page

5   After lunch, I visited the Oceanarium, which showcased Pacific Northwest animals including dolphins, penguins, whales, seals, and sea otters. My favorite spot in this exhibit was the 3 million gallon tank that held Pacific white-sided dolphins and beluga whales. It was so serene watching these beautiful animals swim through the water. I never wanted to leave.

6   Our last stop was the gift store. My father bought me a beluga whale keychain. We left the aquarium and, as I looked back at those giant white pillars, I rubbed the new beluga whale keychain in my pocket. I imagined swimming in the tank with the white-sided dolphins and the beluga whales, swimming serenely alongside the most beautiful creatures I had ever seen. I couldn't help but smile.

---

[1]marine biologist: a person who studies underwater plants and animals

Question **7** *assesses:*

Acquisition of Vocabulary Standard

Benchmark E: Use knowledge of roots and affixes to determine the meanings of complex words.

6. Apply the knowledge of prefixes, suffixes and roots and their various inflections to analyze the meanings of words.

Reading R

7. "When I first arrived at the **aquarium**, I was very excited."

   What is the root of the word **aquarium**?

   A. The root is *rium* and it means *home*.

   B. The root is *rium* and it means *fish*.

   C. The root is *aqua* and it means *animal*.

   D. The root is *aqua* and it means *water*.

Go to next page

Show What You Know® on the OAT — Tutorial

Grade 6 Reading

Reading R

7.   Ⓐ   Ⓑ   Ⓒ   Ⓓ

Go to next page ➡

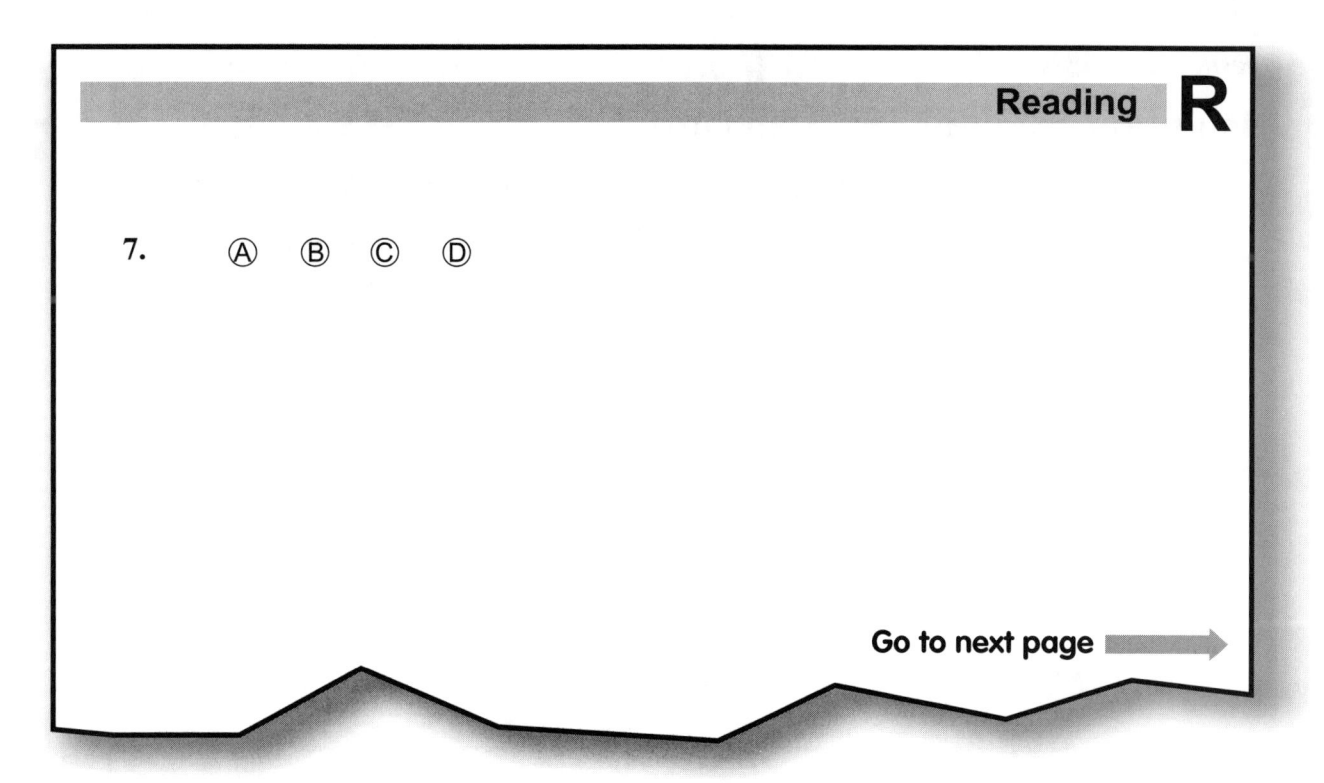

Analysis: *The word aquarium is made up of a root, aqua, and a suffix, rium. The root word aqua means water. Choice D is correct. Choices A and B are incorrect. These answer choices are the suffix of the word aquarium, not the root word. Choice C is incorrect because the root word aqua means water, not animal.*

Tutorial

Show What You Know® on the OAT

Grade 6 Reading

*Question **8** assesses:*

Acquisition of Vocabulary Standard

Benchmark F: Use multiple resources to enhance comprehension of vocabulary.

8. Determine the meanings and pronunciations of unknown words by using dictionaries, thesauruses, glossaries, technology, and textual features, such as definitional footnotes or sidebars.

Reading R

8. In the selection, what does the phrase **marine biologist** mean?

   A. the science of marine life

   B. a person who studies underwater plants and animals

   C. a soldier who works at a marina

   D. the science of fish

Go to next page ➡

Reading

8. Ⓐ Ⓑ Ⓒ Ⓓ

Go to next page →

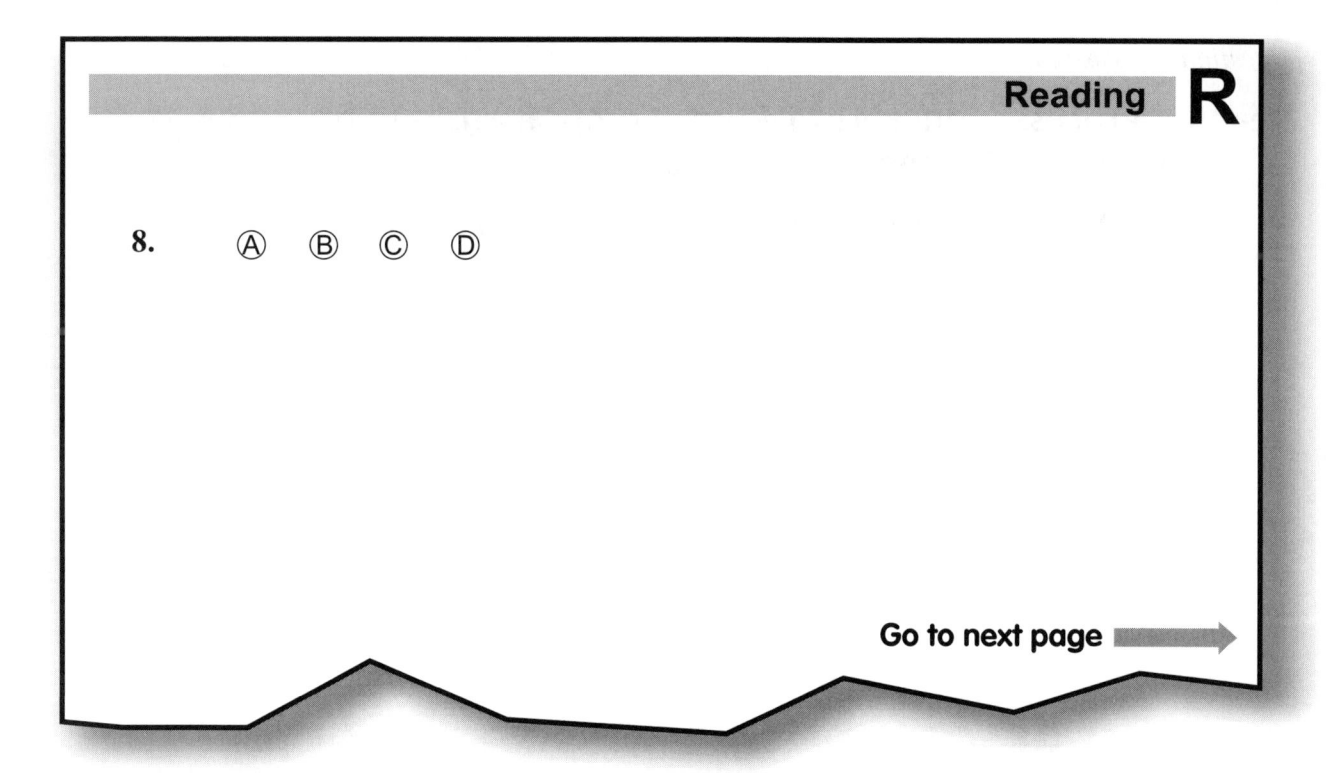

Analysis: A marine biologist is a person who studies underwater plants and animals. This information is given in a definitional footnote. Choice B is correct. Choices A and D are incorrect. The term marine biologist refers to a person, not a science. Choice C is incorrect because it is not the correct definition of a marine biologist. A marine biologist can work with and study underwater plants and animals at many more places than just a marina. Also, the term marine is being used to describe water, not a type of soldier. Choice D is incorrect because marine biologists study much more than just fish.

Question **9** *assesses:*

Reading Process: Concepts of Print, Comprehension Strategies, and Self-Monitoring Strategies Standard

Benchmark A: Determine a purpose for reading and use a range of reading comprehension strategies to better understand text.

1. Establish and adjust purposes for reading, including to find out, to understand, to interpret, to enjoy and to solve problems.

Reading R

9. What are two reasons why the narrator enjoyed the trip to Shedd Aquarium?

   Write your answer in the **Answer Document**. (2 points)

Go to next page

9. Write your response to question 9 in the space below.

_____

Go to next page ➡

Analysis: *Short-answer responses may vary. The narrator enjoyed the trip to Shedd Aquarium because the narrator loves underwater creatures and wants to become a marine biologist. The narrator had also just completed a research paper on animals of the Pacific Ocean for school and was able to see some of the creatures that had been researched.*

Question 10 assesses:

Reading Process: Concepts of Print, Comprehension Strategies, and Self-Monitoring Strategies Standard

Benchmark A: Determine a purpose for reading and use a range of reading comprehension strategies to better understand text.

5. Select, create and use graphic organizers to interpret textual information.

Reading R

10. Look at the timeline below containing the places in Sheed Aquarium that the narrator visited.

| visits the Caribbean Coral Reef exhibit |
| visits Fish From Around the World exhibit |
| eats lunch at the Bubble Net Food Court |
| |
| goes to gift shop |

Which event belongs in the empty box?

A. visits the Oceanarium

B. visits the shark exhibit

C. watches a diver hand feed the fish

D. pets a Pacific Ocean turtle

Go to next page ➡

10. Ⓐ Ⓑ Ⓒ Ⓓ

Go to next page ➡

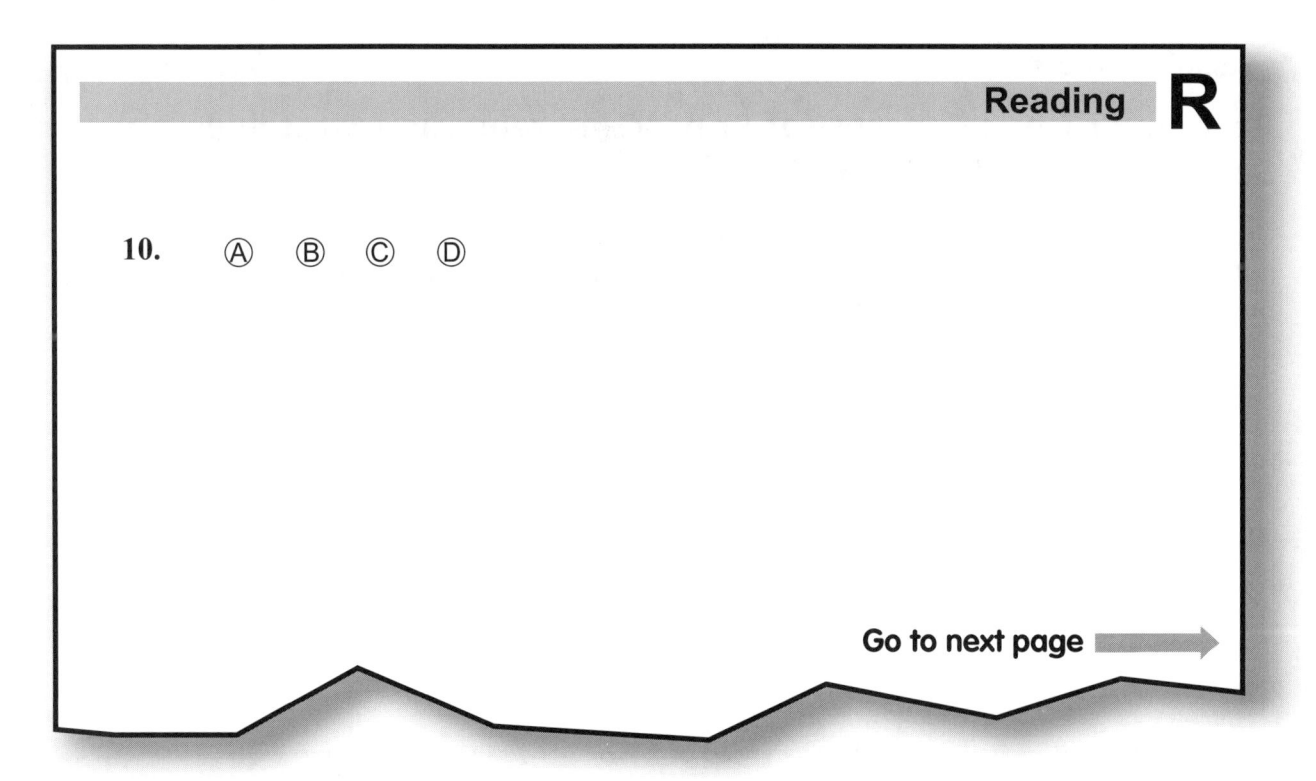

Analysis*: The chart gives the sequence of events of the narrator's day at the aquarium. The correct event that completes this sequence is that the narrator visits the Oceanarium. Choice A is correct. Choices B and D are incorrect. They did not happen in this passage. Choice C is incorrect. This event happens while the narrator visits the Caribbean Coral Reef exhibit.*

Question 11 assesses:

Reading Process: Concepts of Print, Comprehension Strategies, and Self-Monitoring Strategies Standard

Benchmark B: Apply effective reading comprehension strategies, including summarizing and making predictions and comparisons, using information in text, between text and across subject areas.

2. Predict or hypothesize as appropriate from information in the text, substantiating with specific references to textual examples that may be in widely separated sections of text.

Reading R

11. Predict whether the narrator will still become a marine biologist after the trip to Shedd Aquarium. Provide two details from the selection to support your answer.

    Write your answer in the **Answer Document**. (2 points)

Go to next page ➡

11. Write your response to question 11 in the space below.

Analysis: Short-answer responses may vary. I predict that the narrator will become a marine biologist in the future. The narrator wanted to become a marine biologist before going to Shedd Aquarium and had previously researched underwater creatures. At the aquarium, the narrator enjoyed seeing all of the creatures that the narrator had learned about before the trip. The narrator is fascinated by the underwater creatures and will probably become a marine biologist to learn more about them.

Reading

Travel south? Why? Look at all the beautiful snow!
By Sheryl Cooper

1 Every year during December, I am guaranteed to hear the same question: "Are you going to travel south this month?" It drives me crazy! I live in northern Minnesota for a reason. I love the winter.

2 Winter is my favorite season. I know that I may be part of a minority, but I think that people should give winter a fighting chance. The temperatures are freezing, but who doesn't like to come home to a warm house, or wear large soft sweaters everyday, or curl up next to a warm fire with a tall glass of hot chocolate?

3 There are also many activities to do outside when it's cold. There's skiing, snow boarding, ice skating, snow mobiling, ice fishing, hunting, snowman building, snowball fighting, and snow angel making, just to name a few. There are also many indoor activities that can be pursued while staying out of the cold weather. There's not a moment of boredom in the month of December so I don't understand why people leave for warmer climates. They are missing the simple pleasures of the snow that are waiting for them at home.

4 Snow—this is by far the greatest reason why I love the winter so much. When the snow falls, it looks like a whimsical ballet of little white ballerinas floating in the air. It's a magical experience to find yourself caught in a snowfall. It's like someone is shaking up your life's snow globe and you get to experience the magic from the inside. Then after the snowfall, the snow covers everything and makes it sparkle with white and silver diamond radiance.

5 I believe that everyone should experience a northern winter and be excited to do so. It's a magical season full of warmth and love despite the cold temperatures outside. People in northern Minnesota should not be traveling south to warmer weather; the people living in the warmer weather should travel to Minnesota and experience a real winter in all its radiance.

I'm traveling south the second it snows!
By Trevor Wallenski

1   I live in Boston, Massachusetts. I love Boston. I love the summer months when the weather is warm, but not too hot. I love the history in Boston. The one and only thing that I don't like in Boston is the snow, and I plan on taking a long vacation down south once it comes.

2   I wouldn't want to be anywhere else but in Boston during the rest of the year; however, when those icy flakes start falling my love turns to disgust. How could anyone love the frigid temperatures that chill you to the bone? Or enjoy the precariously icy walkways or the slushy, slippery roads? Everything is colder and more dangerous during the winter time. It is not a happy season. It is a season of cold and despair.

3   During the winter, a person's immune system will weaken and he or she will become prone to many more bouts of the cold or flu than during the other seasons of the year. Tissues need to be at hand at all times since the cold weather turns runny noses into the norm.

4   The days are dark and gloomy. Because of the time change, it is dark for more hours during the day in the winter, but down south it is still sunny and warm. Personally, I feel happier when I see more sunlight during each day. I also believe that I eat healthier, drink more water, and generally feel better in warmer weather. Most people will agree when I say that winter is the worst of the seasons and that a nice warm vacation is needed when the snow begins to fall.

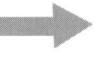

Question **12** *assesses:*

Reading Process: Concepts of Print, Comprehension Strategies, and Self-Monitoring Strategies Standard

Benchmark B: Apply effective reading comprehension strategies, including summarizing and making predictions and comparisons, using information in text, between text and across subject areas.

3. Make critical comparisons across texts, noting author's style as well as literal and implied content of text.

Reading R

12. What is each author's purpose for writing his or her selection?

   A. Both authors persuade the reader to either like or dislike the winter.

   B. Sheryl's selection is persuasive; Trevor's selection is narrative.

   C. Sheryl's selection is poetic; Trevor's selection is expository.

   D. Both authors' wrote narrative selections.

Go to next page

12. Ⓐ Ⓑ Ⓒ Ⓓ

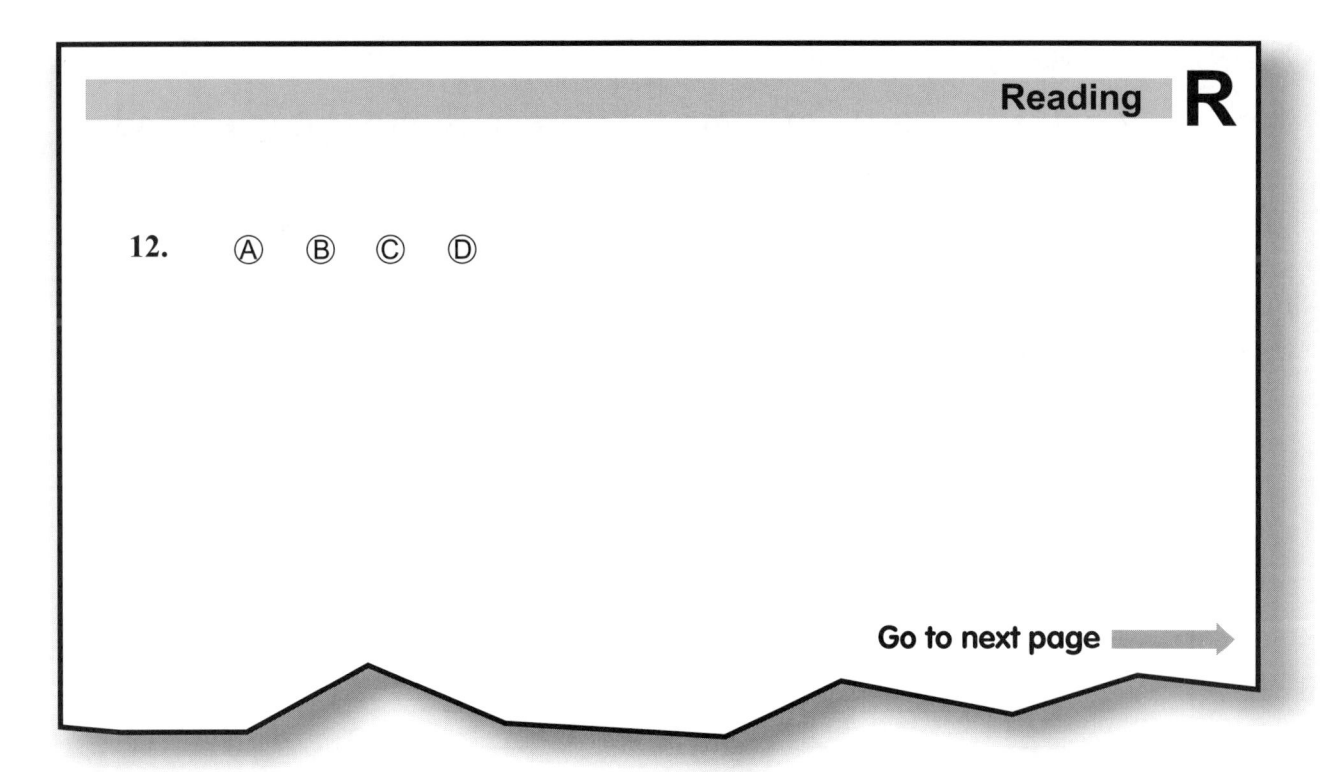

Analysis: Both authors use persuasive devices in their passages to persuade the reader to either like or dislike the winter. Choice A is correct. Choice B is incorrect. Trevor's passage is true, not a narrative story. Choices C and D are incorrect. Both authors wrote about true events in their lives; the information was not fictional.

Question **13** *assesses:*

Reading Process: Concepts of Print, Comprehension Strategies, and Self-Monitoring Strategies Standard

Benchmark B: Apply effective reading comprehension strategies, including summarizing and making predictions and comparisons, using information in text, between text and across subject areas.

4. Summarize the information in texts, recognizing important ideas and supporting details, and noting gaps or contradictions.

Reading

13. Summarize the two selections. Use two examples from each selection in your answer.

    Write your answer in the **Answer Document**. (4 points)

Go to next page

13. Write your response to question 13 in the space below.

Analysis: Extended-response answers may vary. Sheryl believes that people should like the winter because there are many fun activities to do outside in the cold weather. She also believes that snow is beautiful, and she thinks that everyone should think that snow is beautiful. Trevor believes that people should not like the winter because the walkways become icy and the roads become slippery. He also said that people are more prone to getting sick during the winter because their immune systems are weakened.

Question **14** *assesses:*

Reading Process: Concepts of Print, Comprehension Strategies, and Self-Monitoring Strategies Standard

Benchmark C: Make meaning through asking and responding to a variety of questions related to text.

6. Answer literal, inferential, evaluative and synthesizing questions to demonstrate comprehension of grade-appropriate print texts, and electronic and visual media.

Reading R

14. Evaluate each author's argument. Which author makes the better argument? Use two examples from the text to support your answer.

    Write your answer in the **Answer Document**. (2 points)

Go to next page

Reading R

14. Write your response to question 14 in the space below.

Analysis: Short-answer responses may vary. I think that Trevor makes a stronger argument because he states more examples of why people should dislike the winter than Sheryl's passage states about why people should like the winter. Trevor says that most people believe his argument so that probably means that it is a strong one. I agree with Trevor when he says that the winter is dark and gloomy because it's dark outside more often and everything is cold—too cold.

Question **15** *assesses:*

Reading Process: Concepts of Print, Comprehension Strategies, and Self-Monitoring Strategies Standard

Benchmark D: Apply self-monitoring strategies to clarify confusion about text and to monitor comprehension.

7. Monitor own comprehension by adjusting speed to fit the purpose, or by skimming, scanning, reading on, looking back, note taking or summarizing what has been read so far in text.

Reading R

15. Look back at Sheryl's selection. What does she describe as being "full of warmth and love despite the cold temperatures"?

    A. the snow

    B. the winter

    C. a sleigh ride

    D. a house

15. Ⓐ Ⓑ Ⓒ Ⓓ

Reading

Go to next page

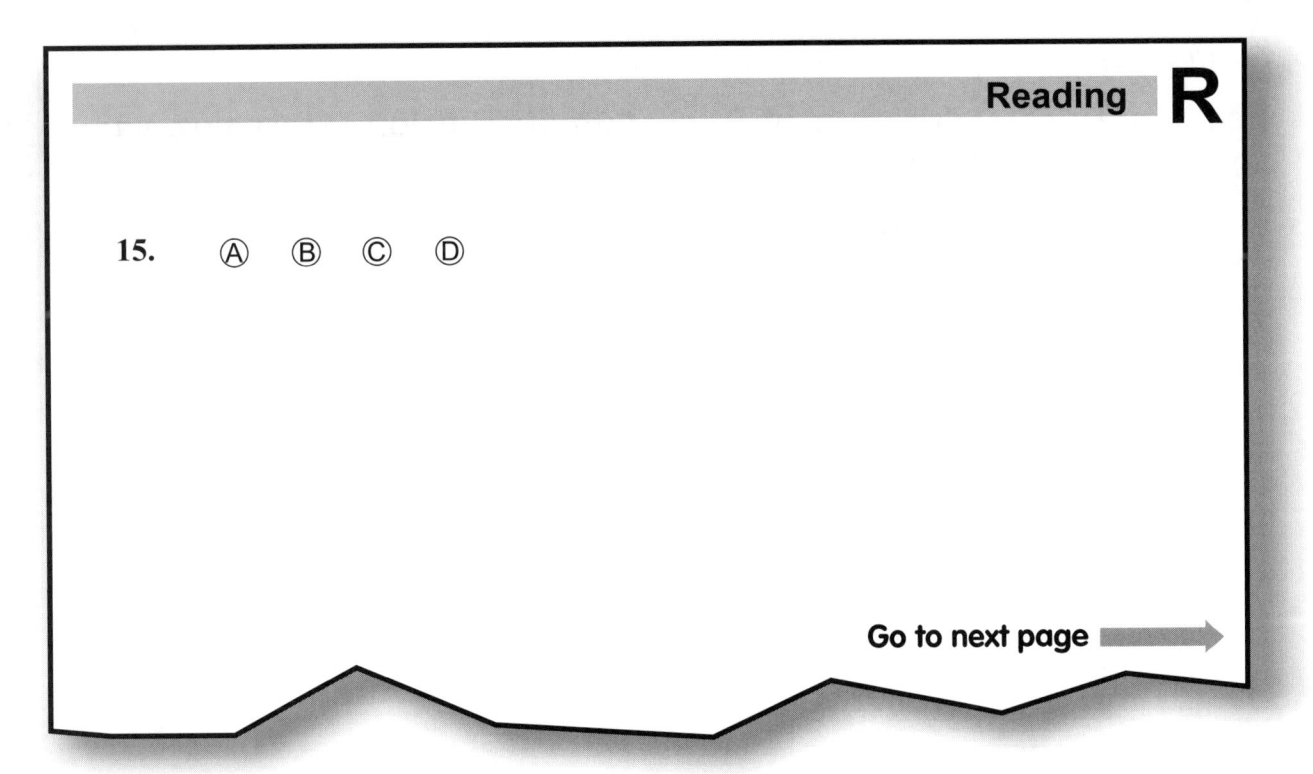

Analysis: Sheryl describes the winter as being "full of warmth and love despite the cold temperatures." Choice B is correct. Choice A, C, and D are incorrect. Sheryl did not mention these choices as being full of warmth and love in the passage.

Question **16** *assesses:*

Reading Process: Concepts of Print, Comprehension Strategies, and Self-Monitoring Strategies Standard

Benchmark D: Apply self-monitoring strategies to clarify confusion about text and to monitor comprehension.

8. List questions and search for answers within the text to construct meaning.

Reading

16. How does Trevor describe walkways during the winter?

   A. He says they are covered in salt that gets on your shoes and clothes.

   B. He says they are beautiful when they are covered with snow.

   C. He says they are slushy and slippery.

   D. He says they are precariously icy.

16. Ⓐ Ⓑ Ⓒ Ⓓ

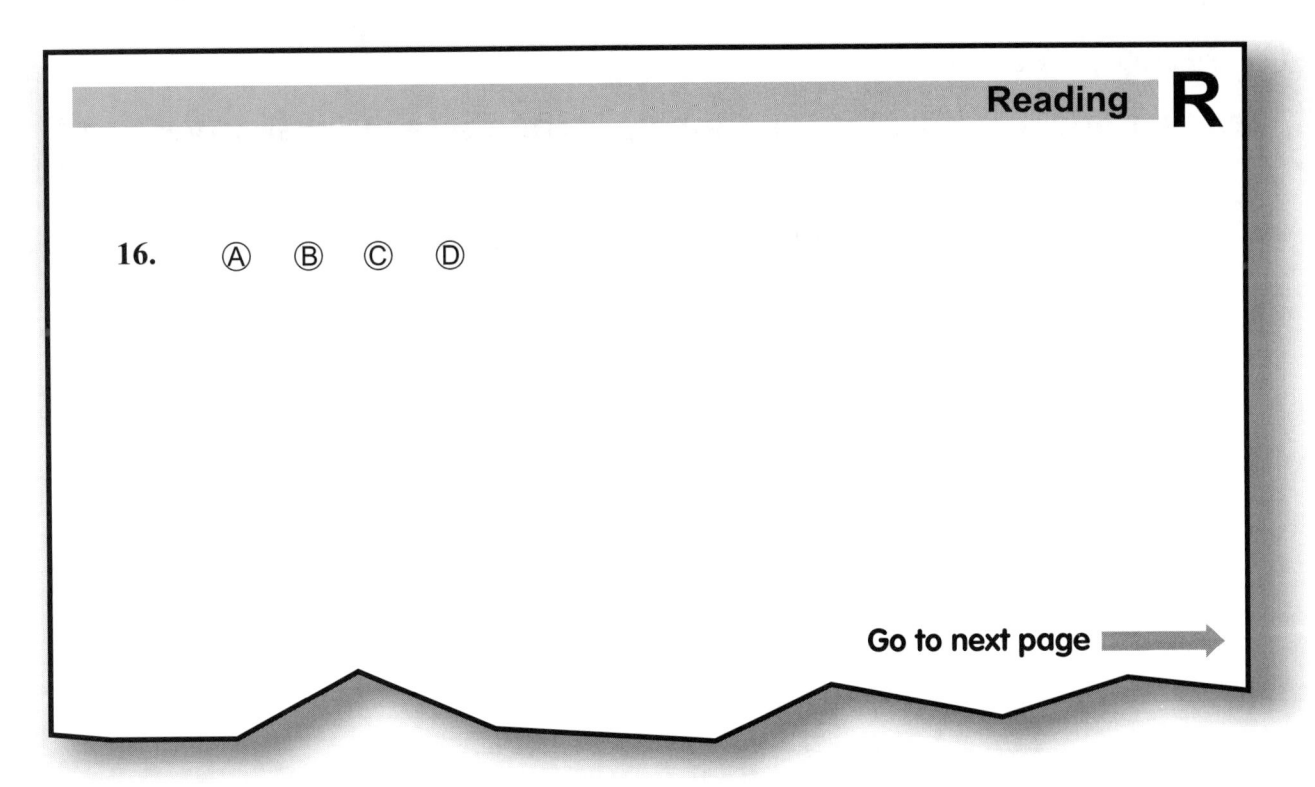

Analysis: Trevor describes the walkways during the winter as precariously icy. Choice D is correct. Choice A is incorrect; Trevor does not mention salt on your shoes or clothes in his selection. Choice B is incorrect because Trevor does not like the winter or the snow. Choice C is incorrect because this description is what Trevor says about roads in the winter, not the walkways.

Question 17 assesses:

Reading Applications: Informational, Technical, and Persuasive Text Standard

Benchmark A: Use text features and graphics to organize, analyze and draw inferences from content and to gain additional information.

1. Use text features, such as chapter titles, headings and subheading; parts of books, including index, appendix, table of contents and online tools (search engines) to locate information.

Reading R

17. What does each selection's title tell you about the author's point of view on winter?

    A. Sheryl's title tells the reader that she likes the seasons, and Trevor's title tells the reader that he dislikes the seasons.

    B. Sheryl's title tells the reader that she likes snow, and Trevor's title tells the reader that he plans to travel south once the snow begins to fall.

    C. Sheryl's title tells the reader that she likes to ice skate, and Trevor's title tells the reader that he likes to surf.

    D. Sheryl's title tells the reader that she does not like the winter, and Trevor's title tells the reader that he does like the winter.

Go to next page

17. Ⓐ Ⓑ Ⓒ Ⓓ

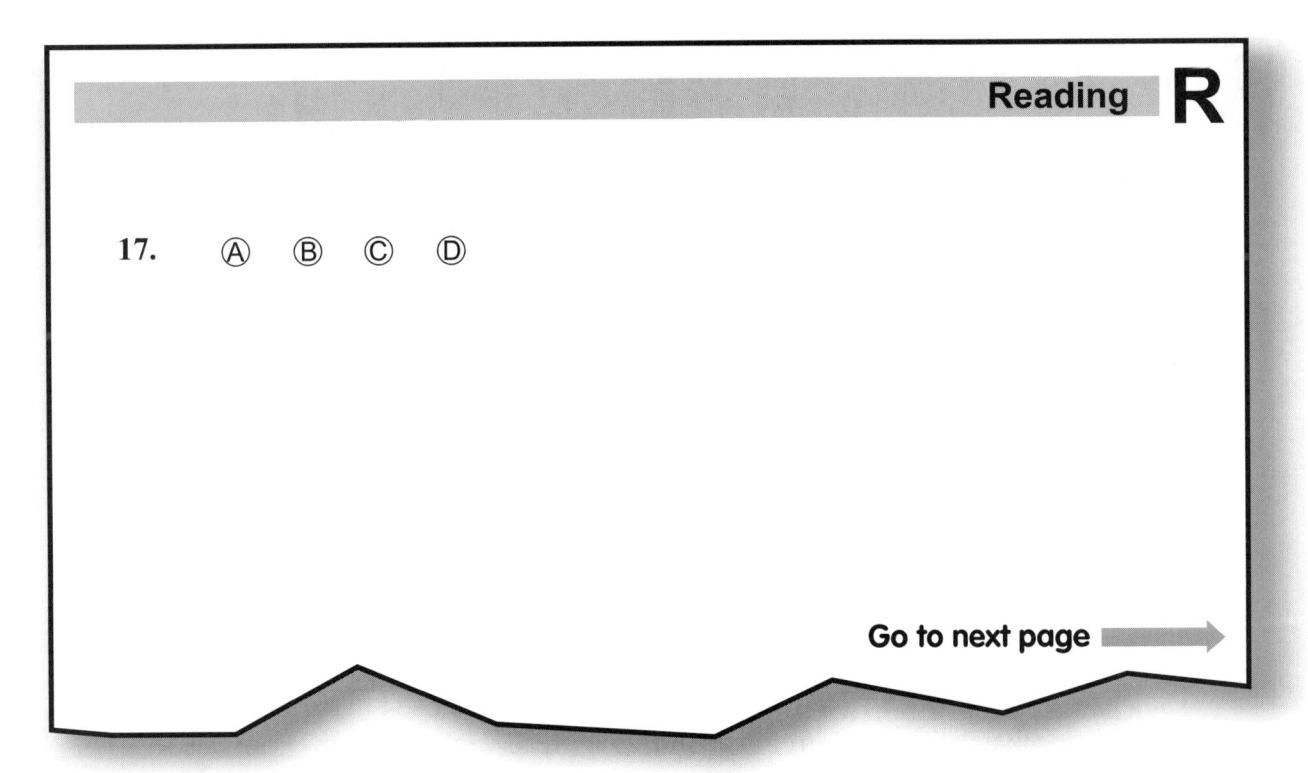

Go to next page →

Analysis: Sheryl's title tells the reader that she likes snow; it says, "Travel south? Why? Look at all the beautiful snow!" Trevor's title tells the reader that he plans to travel south once the snow begins to fall. It says, "I'm traveling south the second it snows!" Choice B is correct. Choice A is incorrect because both titles talk about the snow, not seasons in general. Choice C is incorrect; the titles do not mention ice skating or surfing. Choice D is incorrect. This is the opposite of how the titles describe each author's passage.

Reading

Fungus Bread

1   Claudia is learning about microorganisms in her science class. She learns that bacteria, viruses, protists, archaea, and fungi are all microorganisms. Claudia's teacher separates the class into five different groups and assigns each group to write a paper about their assigned microorganism. Claudia's group must research fungi.

2   Her group researches fungi and finds this description in an encyclopedia:

3   *A fungus is a eukaryotic organism that digests its food externally and absorbs the nutrient molecules into its cells. Fungi were originally grouped with plants, but researchers found out that fungi are actually more closely related to animals. Following this discovery, fungi were placed into their own group. They play a very important role in most ecosystems and they do more good than bad for the other organisms in the world.*

4   Claudia's group also learns that a fungus has its DNA enclosed in its nucleus. Unlike plants that receive their energy from the sun, fungi receive their energy from dead organisms. Fungi include single-celled creatures—the yeasts—and multicellular creatures, such as molds or mushrooms.

5   Fungi grow best in environments that are slightly acidic (a pH measurement of 5 or so; a pH of 7 is neutral). They also can grow on substances with very low moisture. Fungi live in the soil and on your body, in your house and on plants and animals, in freshwater and seawater. A single teaspoon of topsoil contains about 120,000 fungi.

6   Fungi can be good, such as fungi that doctors use to make antibiotics that fight off bacterial diseases. The drug penicillin is an antibiotic created from a fungus. Some fungi can be bad, such as the mold that grows on fruit and bread.

7   In order to learn more about fungi, Claudia's group decides to conduct an experiment to grow mold on bread. The group finds information on how to conduct the experiment and they begin.

8   They get three eyedroppers, sugar water, lemon juice, tap water, four slices of white bread, four resealable sandwich bags, a marker, and masking tape to conduct their experiment.

9   The group puts one piece of bread into a sandwich bag and labels it "Dry Bread." Then they drop sugar water over the next slice, put it in the bag, and label it "Sugar Water on Bread." They drop tap water on the third slice and lemon juice on the fourth slice, put them in bags, and label them as well. Then the group puts the bags in a closet that is warm and dark—a perfect place to grow fungus. Claudia predicts that the tap water bread will grow the least amount of fungus because there is a small amount of chlorine in it. She predicts that the sugar water bread will grow the most mold because it's full of carbohydrate energy.

10 Each day Claudia's group checks the bags and records how much fungus has grown on each piece of bread. After two weeks, here's what the group finds:

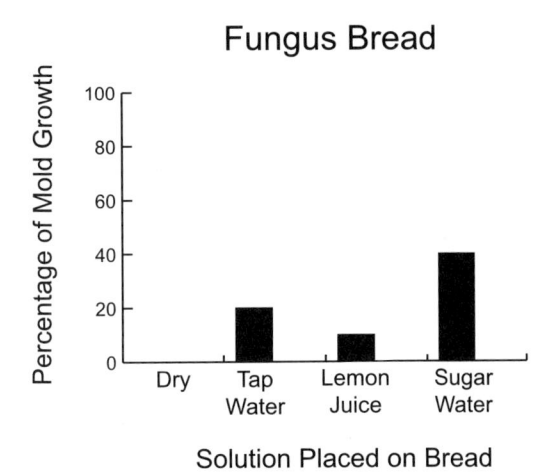

Fungus Bread

Solution Placed on Bread	Percentage of Mold Growth
Dry	0
Tap Water	20
Lemon Juice	10
Sugar Water	40

11 Claudia's group turns in their paper and the results from their experiment to their teacher and receives a very good grade for all the hard work that they put into their assignment.

Tutorial

Show What You Know® on the OAT

Grade 6 Reading

Question **18** *assesses:*

Reading Applications: Informational, Technical, and Persuasive Text Standard

Benchmark A: Use text features and graphics to organize, analyze and draw inferences from content and to gain additional information.

5. Analyze information found in maps, charts, tables, graphs, diagrams and cutaways.

Reading R

18. According to the information in the graph, what bread grew the most mold and what bread grew the least mold?

   A. The lemon juice bread grew the most mold, and the dry bread grew the least mold.

   B. The dry bread grew the most mold, and the tap water bread grew the least mold.

   C. The tap water bread grew the most mold, and the sugar water bread grew the least mold.

   D. The sugar water bread grew the most mold, and the dry bread grew the least mold.

Go to next page

18. Ⓐ Ⓑ Ⓒ Ⓓ

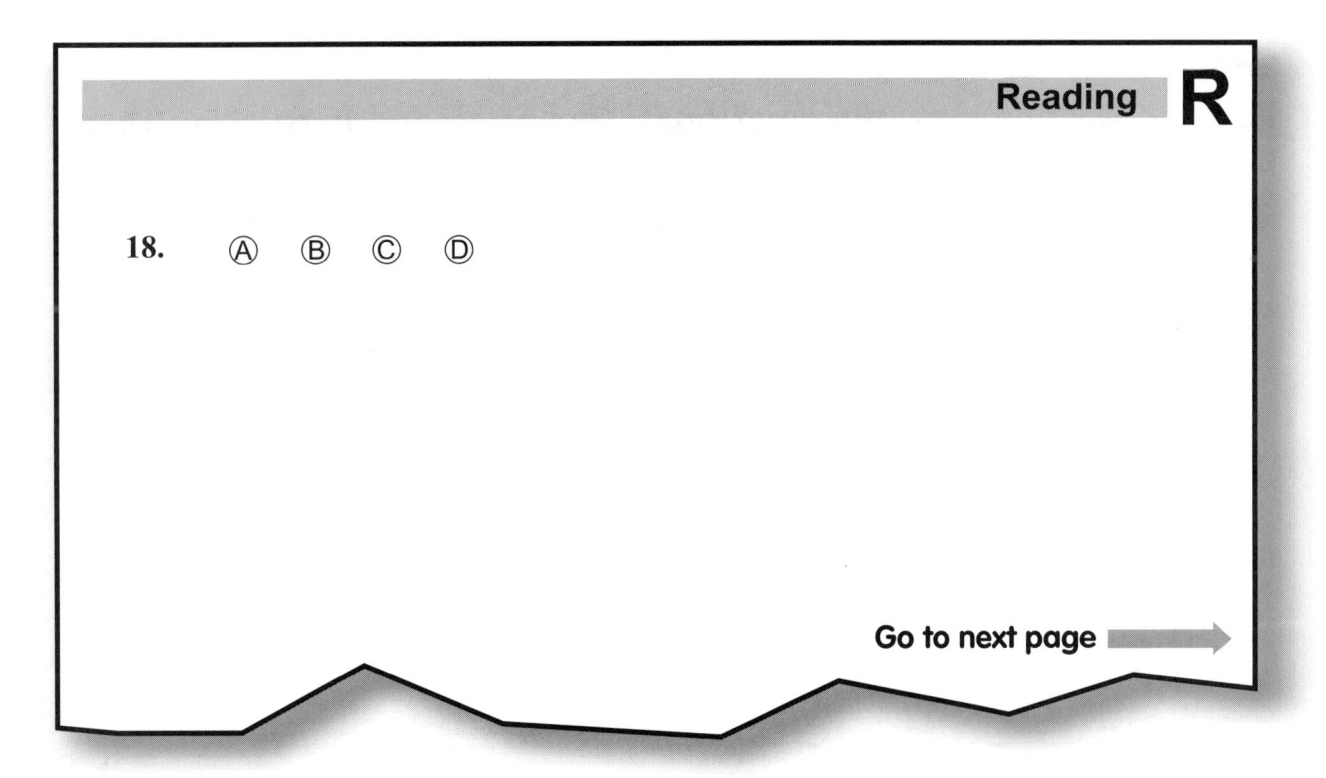

Go to next page ▶

Analysis: According to the graph, the sugar water bread grew the most mold (40% of the bread was covered), and the dry bread grew the least mold (0% of the bread was covered). Choice D is correct. Choices A, B, and C are incorrect. They do not represent the information given on the graph.

Question **19** *assesses:*

Reading Applications: Informational, Technical, and Persuasive Text Standard

Benchmark B: Recognize the difference between cause and effect and fact and opinion to analyze text.

2. Analyze examples of cause and effect and fact and opinion.

Reading

19. In the experiment that Claudia's group conducts, what causes the mold to grow?

A. sunlight and moist bread in a cool environment

B. sunlight and dry bread in a warm environment

C. darkness and moist bread in a warm environment

D. darkness and moist bread in a cool environment

Go to next page

19. Ⓐ Ⓑ Ⓒ Ⓓ

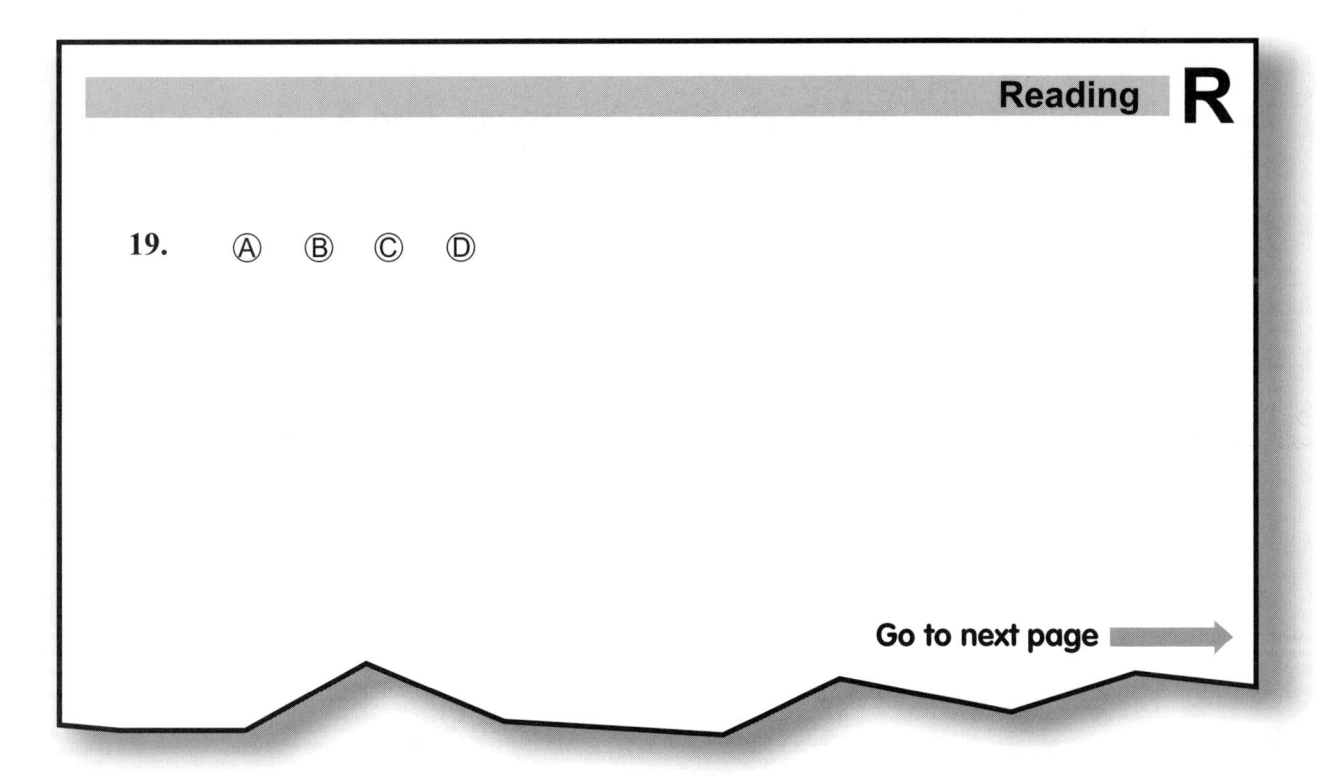

Go to next page ➡

Analysis: In order for the mold to grow, the bread had to be moist and in a dark, warm environment. Choice C correctly uses information given in the passage to understand cause and effect. Choices A, B, and D are incorrect. These answer choices misinterpret information in the passage to understand cause and effect.

Question **20** *assesses:*

Reading Applications: Informational, Technical, and Persuasive Text Standard

Benchmark C: Explain how main ideas connect to each other in a variety of sources.

3. Compare and contrast important details about a topic, using different sources of information, including books, magazines, newspapers and online resources.

Reading

20. How is the encyclopedia information in paragraph 3 similar to the information about plants and fungi in paragraph 4?

    A. Both paragraphs describe how fungi are different than plants.

    B. Both paragraphs describe the similar reproductive systems of plants and fungi.

    C. Both paragraphs describe how plants are similar to fungi.

    D. Both paragraphs describe how plants and fungi defend themselves from predators.

Go to next page

Reading R

20. Ⓐ Ⓑ Ⓒ Ⓓ

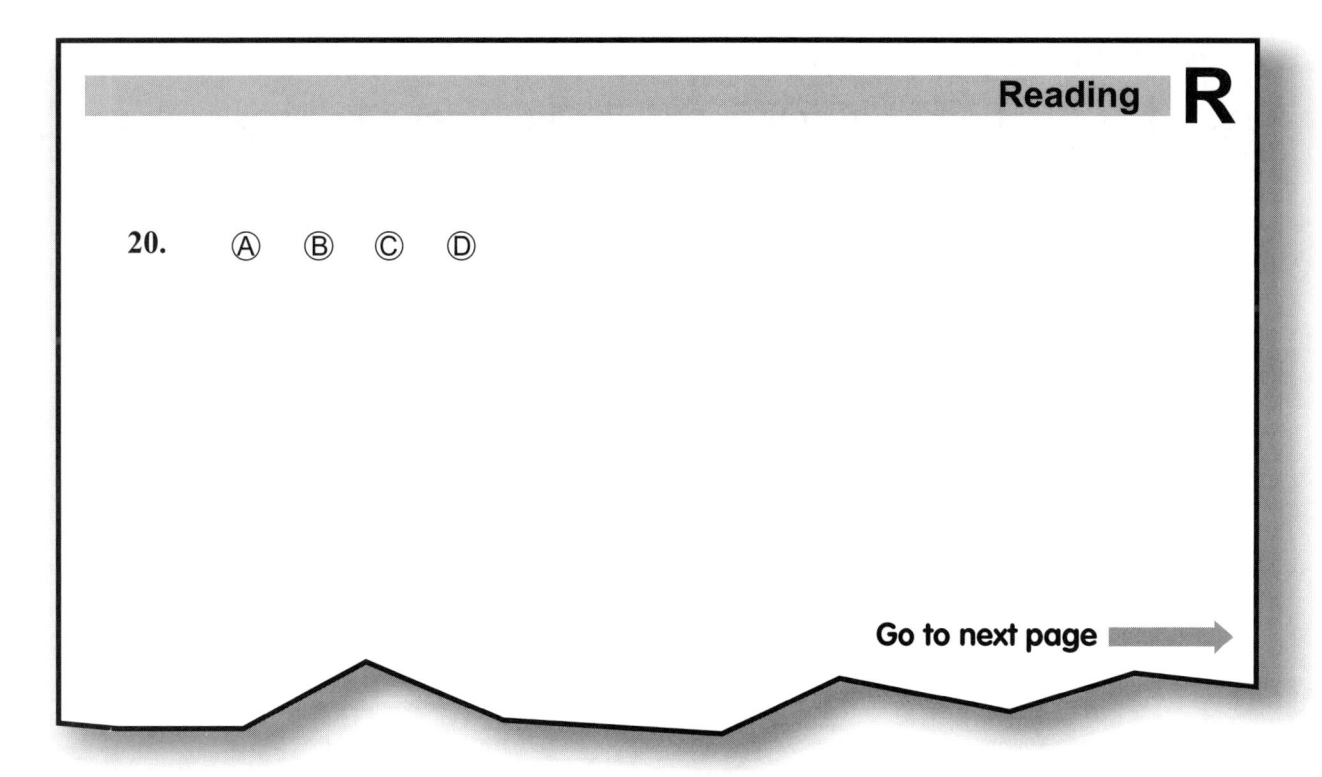

Go to next page ➡

Analysis: Paragraph 3 and paragraph 4 describe how fungi are different than plants. They talk about how they are classified into two different groups and that they receive their energy from different sources. Choice A is correct. Choices B, C, and D are incorrect. This information does not appear in the paragraphs.

Question **21** *assesses:*

Reading Applications: Informational, Technical, and Persuasive Text Standard

Benchmark D: Identify arguments and persuasive techniques used in informational text.

6. Identify an author's argument or viewpoint and assess the adequacy and accuracy of details used.

Reading R

21. Claudia predicts that the tap water bread will grow the least amount of fungus because there is a small amount of chlorine in it. The experiment results show that dry bread grew the least amount of fungus and that tap water bread grew the second highest amount of mold.

    What could explain the inaccuracy of Claudia's prediction?

    A. Claudia's prediction was inaccurate because there is no chlorine in tap water, which is dirty and not purified.

    B. Claudia's prediction was inaccurate because she did not know that tap water contains just as many fungi as the topsoil outside, about 120,000.

    C. Claudia's prediction was inaccurate because she neglected to assume that even with the chlorine, there were other contaminants in the water that would grow mold.

    D. Claudia's prediction was inaccurate because she assumed that there was sugar in the tap water that would make the bread grow a lot of fungus.

    Go to next page ▶

21. Ⓐ Ⓑ Ⓒ Ⓓ

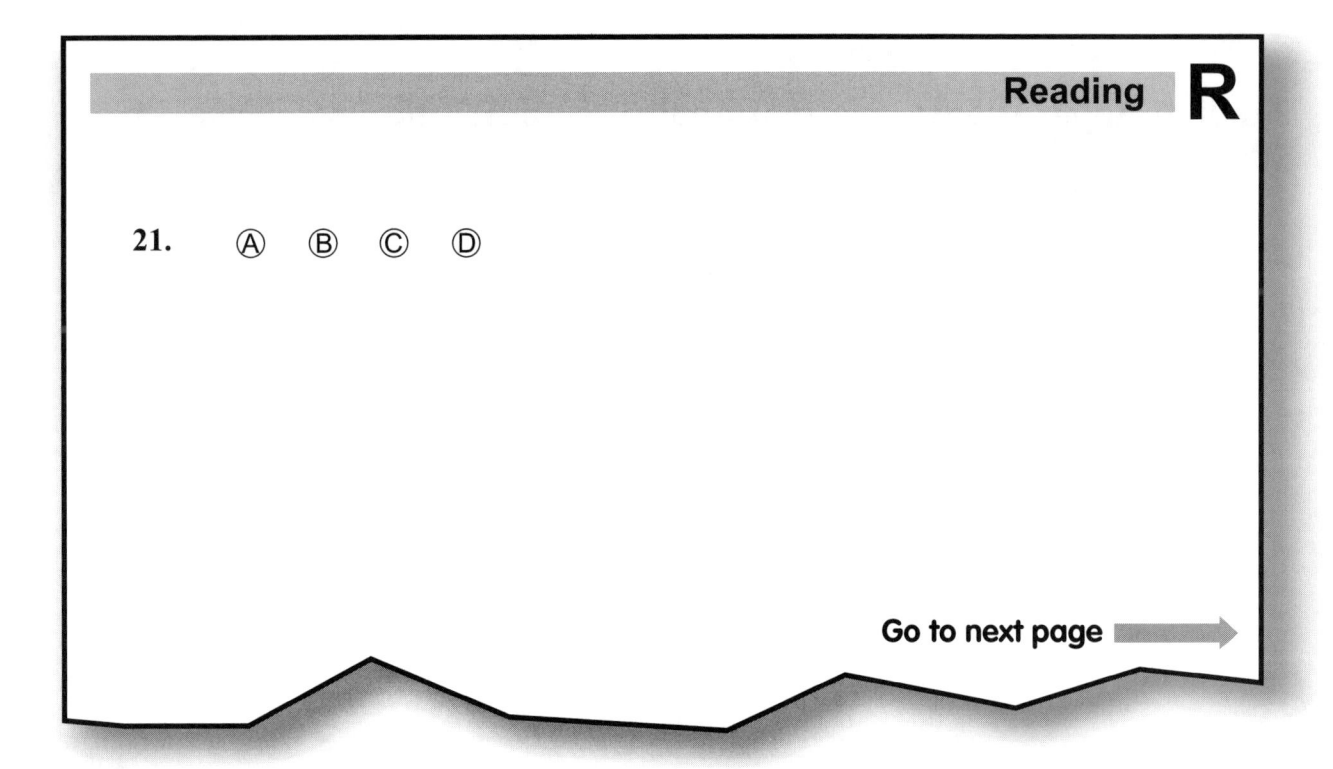

Analysis: Claudia's prediction was inaccurate because she neglected to assume that even with the chlorine there were other contaminants in the water that would grow mold. This answer uses information from the passage and logical analysis to come to the correct conclusion. Choice C is correct. Choice A is incorrect. Tap water is purified with chlorine during water-purification treatments. Choice B is incorrect. If this were true, the tap water bread would grow more fungus than the sugar water bread. Choice D is incorrect. This choice says that she thought tap water would grow the most amount of fungus, which contradicts information in the passage.

Question **22** *assesses:*

Reading Applications: Informational, Technical, and Persuasive Text Standard

Benchmark D: Identify arguments and persuasive techniques used in informational text.

7. Identify and understand an author's purpose for writing, including to explain, entertain, persuade or inform.

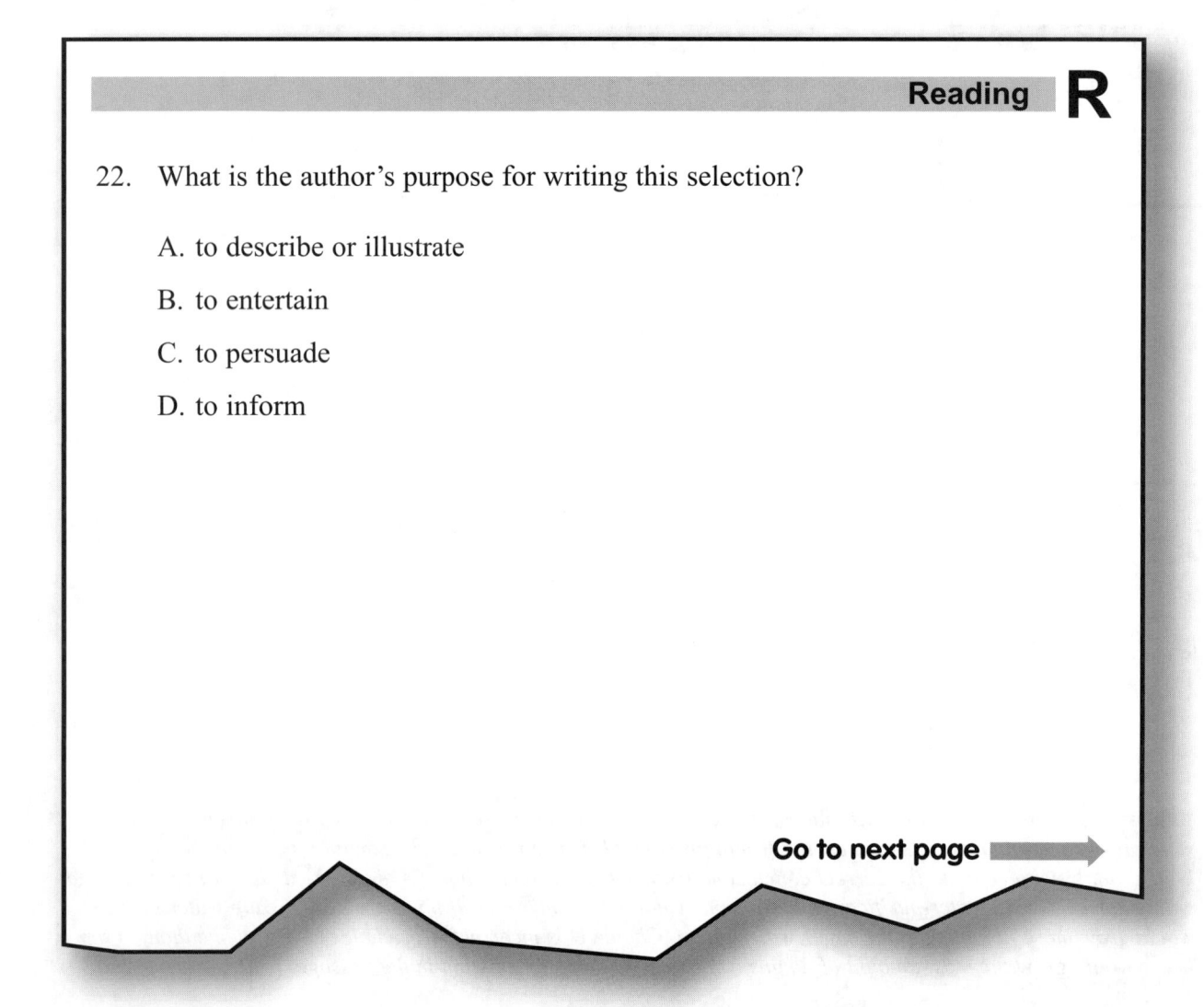

Reading R

22. What is the author's purpose for writing this selection?

　　A. to describe or illustrate

　　B. to entertain

　　C. to persuade

　　D. to inform

Go to next page

22. Ⓐ Ⓑ Ⓒ Ⓓ

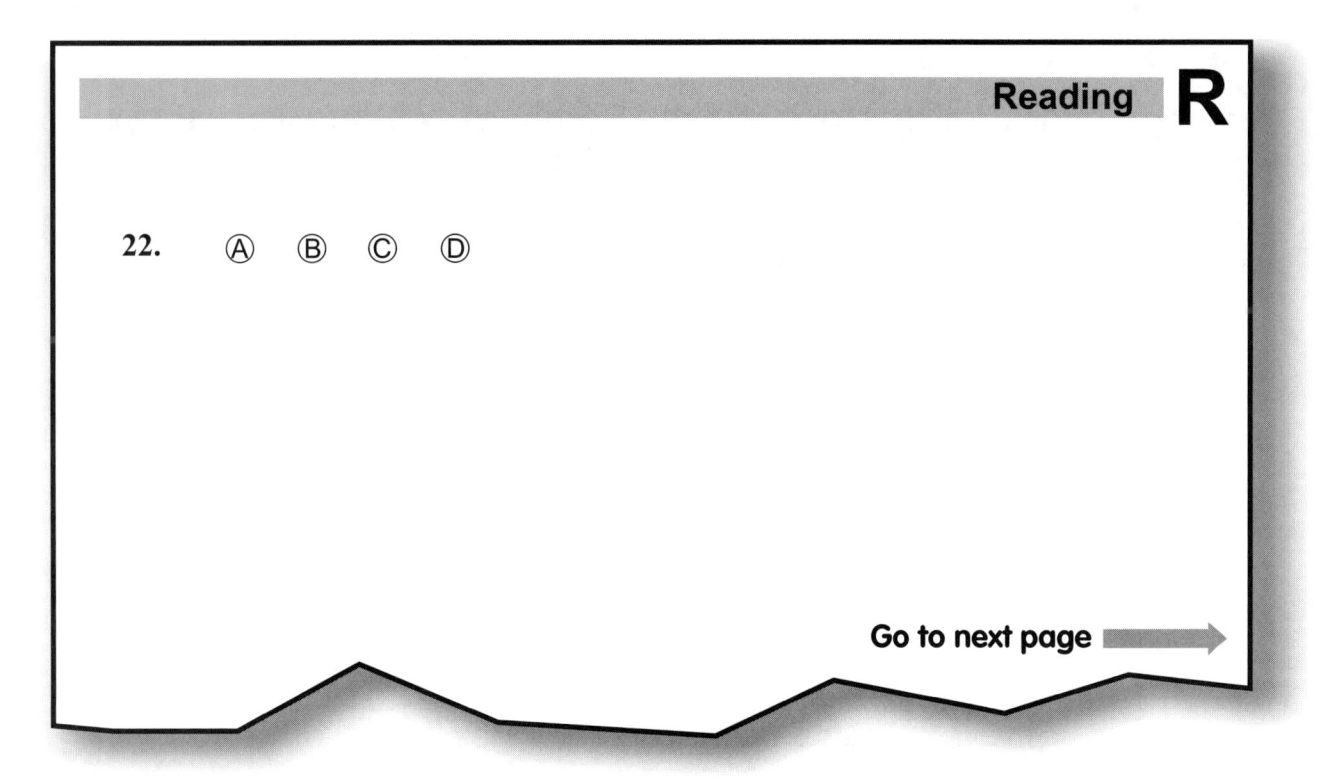

Go to next page ▶

Analysis: The author wrote the passage "Fungus Bread" to inform the reader about the fungus microorganism and what causes it to grow. Choice D is correct. Choice A is incorrect. The author does not provide enough details to enable the reader to recreate the experiment exactly. For instance, the author does not tell the reader exactly how much of each solution was dropped onto the bread. Choice B is incorrect. This passage is not meant to entertain. Choice C is incorrect. This passage does not use persuasive devices.

Question **23** *assesses:*

Reading Applications: Informational, Technical, and Persuasive Text Standard

Benchmark F: Determine the extent to which a summary accurately reflects the main idea, critical details and underlying meaning of original text.

4. Compare original text to a summary to determine the extent to which the summary adequately reflects the main ideas and critical details of the original text.

Reading R

23. Read the following summary of the selection "Fungus Bread."

    Claudia is writing a research paper on fungi for her science class. She and her group decide to conduct an experiment to better understand how and why fungi grow. They grow mold on bread and record their results everyday for two weeks. The results show that dry bread grew the least mold and that sugar water bread grew the most mold. Claudia's group turns in their project and get a good grade for all the hard work that they put into it.

    Is this an accurate summary of the selection? Use two examples from the selection to support your answer.

    Write your answer in the **Answer Document**. (2 points)

    Go to next page ➡

23. Write your response to question 23 in the space below.

Analysis: Short-answer responses may vary. The summary adequately reflects the main ideas and details in the original passage. It covers all of the main events, such as when Claudia is assigned fungi to research for her science class, how Claudia's group conducts the experiment to grow mold on bread, and what the experiment's results are.

Tutorial

Show What You Know® on the OAT

Grade 6 Reading

Question **24** *assesses:*

Reading Applications: Informational, Technical, and Persuasive Text Standard

Benchmark F: Determine the extent to which a summary accurately reflects the main idea, critical details and underlying meaning of original text.

8. Summarize information from informational text, identifying the treatment, scope, and organization of ideas.

Reading R

24. Which is the correct order of main ideas from the selection "Fungus Bread"?

   A. Claudia is assigned fungi to research; she gathers information; she conducts an experiment; she records the results; and she receives a good grade.

   B. Claudia gathers information; she conducts an experiment; she records the results; she is assigned fungi to research; and she receives a good grade.

   C. Claudia is assigned fungi to research; she gathers information; she records the results; she conducts an experiment; and she receives a good grade.

   D. Claudia conducts an experiment; she records the results; she is assigned fungi to research; she gathers information; and she receives a good grade.

Go to next page ➡

Show What You Know® on the OAT — Tutorial

Grade 6 Reading

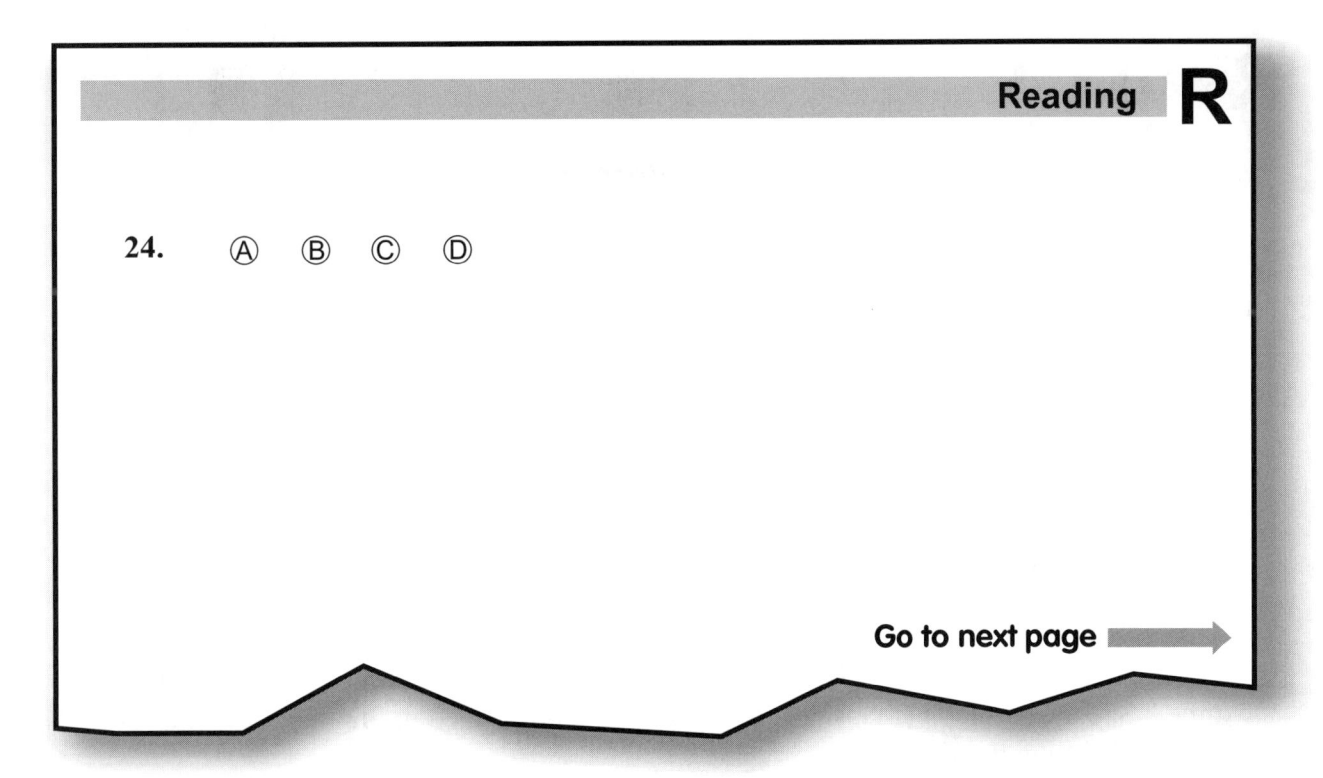

Reading R

24. Ⓐ Ⓑ Ⓒ Ⓓ

Go to next page ➡

Analysis: The correct order of main ideas from the passage is: Claudia is assigned fungi to research; she gathers information; she conducts an experiment; she records the results; and she receives a good grade. Choice A is correct. Choices B, C, and D are incorrect. These answer choices do not exhibit the correct order of main ideas in the passage.

Reading

Little Women
by Louisa May Alcott

1   "Christmas won't be Christmas without any presents," grumbled Jo, lying on the rug.

2   "It's so dreadful to be poor!" sighed Meg, looking down at her old dress.

3   "I don't think it's fair for some girls to have plenty of pretty things, and other girls nothing at all," added little Amy, with an injured sniff.

4   "We've got Father and Mother, and each other," said Beth contentedly from her corner.

5   The four young faces on which the firelight shone brightened at the cheerful words, but darkened again as Jo said sadly, "We haven't got Father, and shall not have him for a long time." She didn't say "perhaps never," but each silently added it, thinking of Father far away, where the fighting was.

6   Nobody spoke for a minute; then Meg said in an altered tone, "You know the reason Mother proposed not having any presents this Christmas was because it is going to be a hard winter for everyone; and she thinks we ought not to spend money for pleasure, when our men are suffering so in the army. We can't do much, but we can make our little sacrifices, and ought to do it gladly. But I am afraid I don't," and Meg shook her head, as she thought regretfully of all the pretty things she wanted.

7   "But I don't think the little we should spend would do any good. We've each got a dollar, and the army wouldn't be much helped by our giving that. I agree not to expect anything from Mother or you, but I do want to buy *Undine and Sintran* for myself. I've wanted it so long," said Jo, who was a bookworm.

8   "I planned to spend mine in new music," said Beth, with a little sigh, which no one heard but the hearth brush and kettle-holder.

9   "I shall get a nice box of Faber's drawing pencils; I really need them," said Amy decidedly.

10   "Mother didn't say anything about our money, and she won't wish us to give up everything. Let's each buy what we want, and have a little fun; I'm sure we work hard enough to earn it," cried Jo, examining the heels of her shoes in a gentlemanly manner.

Question **25** *assesses:*

Reading Applications: Literary Text Standard

Benchmark A: Describe and analyze the elements of character development.

1. Analyze the techniques authors use to describe characters, including narrator or other characters' point of view; character's own thoughts, words or actions.

Reading R

25. How is Beth's reaction to the news that no one will receive presents for Christmas different from the reactions of the other girls? Provide two details from the selection to support your answer.

    Write your answer in the **Answer Document**. (2 points)

25. Write your response to question 25 in the space below.

Go to next page ➡

Analysis: Short-answer responses may vary. The other sisters complain about not receiving presents for Christmas, but Beth remains optimistic and says that she is thankful for her family. When the other girls are openly angry about the news that they will not receive presents, Beth quietly complains to the fireplace so that no one can hear her.

Question **26** *assesses:*

Reading Applications: Literary Text Standard

Benchmark B: Analyze the importance of setting.

2. Identify the features of setting and explain their importance in literary text.

Reading **R**

26. Which setting feature is associated with the changing mood in the girls' conversation?

 A. the snowstorm outside

 B. the firelight

 C. the sunlight

 D. the temperature of the room

26. Ⓐ Ⓑ Ⓒ Ⓓ

Go to next page ▶

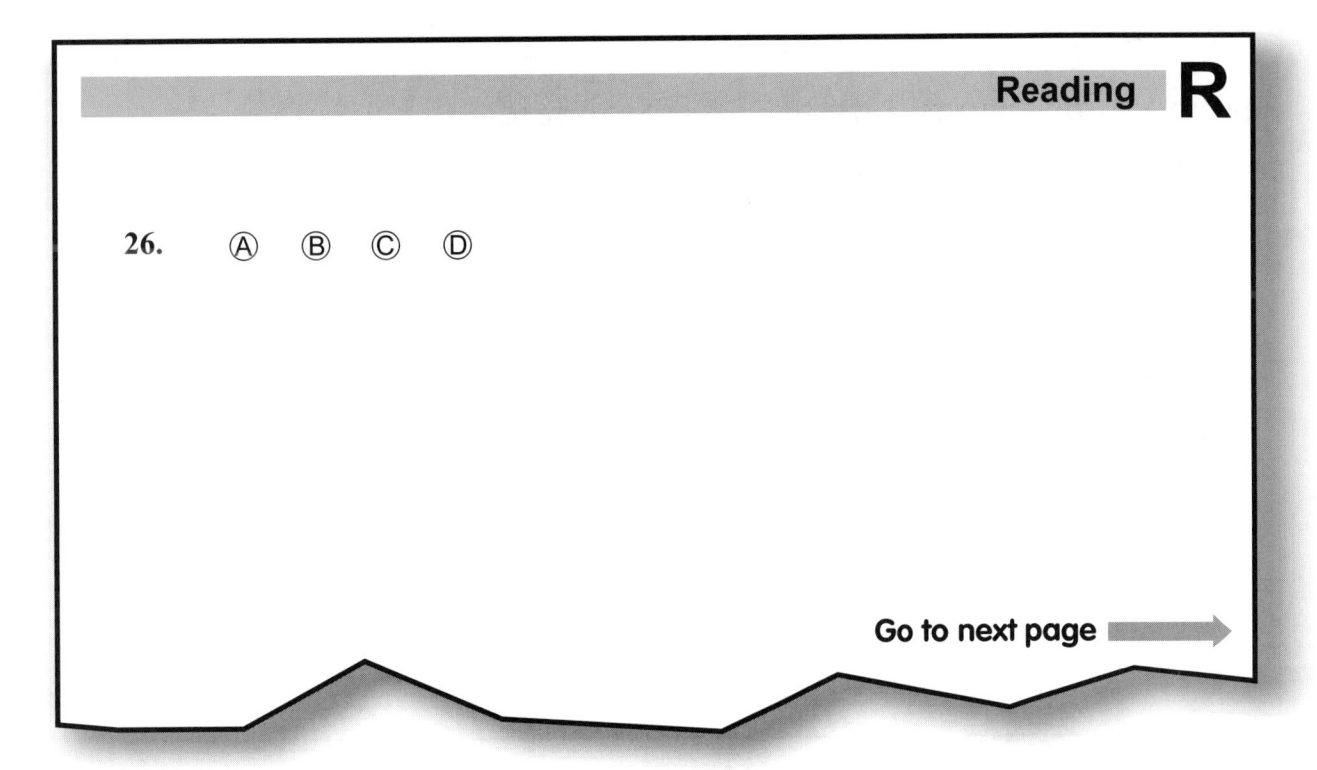

Analysis: *The firelight shined on the girls faces, which brightened when the mood was happy and darkened when the mood became sad. Choice B is correct. Choices A, C, and D are incorrect. These answer choices do not appear in the selection.*

Question **27** *assesses:*

Reading Applications: Literary Text Standard

Benchmark C: Identify the elements of plot and establish a connection between an element and a future event.

3. Identify the main and minor events of the plot, and explain how each incident gives rise to the next.

Reading R

27. What are the two reasons that Jo gives to argue that each girl should be able to buy herself a present if she will not receive presents from anyone else? Use information from the selection to support your answer.

    Write your answer in the **Answer Document**. (2 points)

Go to next page

27. Write your response to question 27 in the space below.

Analysis: Short-answer responses may vary. Jo argues that each girl should be able to buy herself a present for Christmas if she will not receive presents from anyone else. The girls have very little money, a dollar each, and it wouldn't be enough to help the troops. The girls have worked hard for their money and they deserve a present as a reward for it.

Question **28** *assesses:*

Reading Applications: Literary Text Standard

Benchmark D: Differentiate between the points of view in narrative text.

4. Explain first, third, and omniscient points of view, and explain how voice affects the text.

Reading R

28. "She didn't say 'perhaps never,' but each silently added it, thinking of Father far away, where the fighting was."

    What point of view does the sentence above illustrate?

    A. first person

    B. second person

    C. third person

    D. omniscient

Go to next page

28. Ⓐ Ⓑ Ⓒ Ⓓ

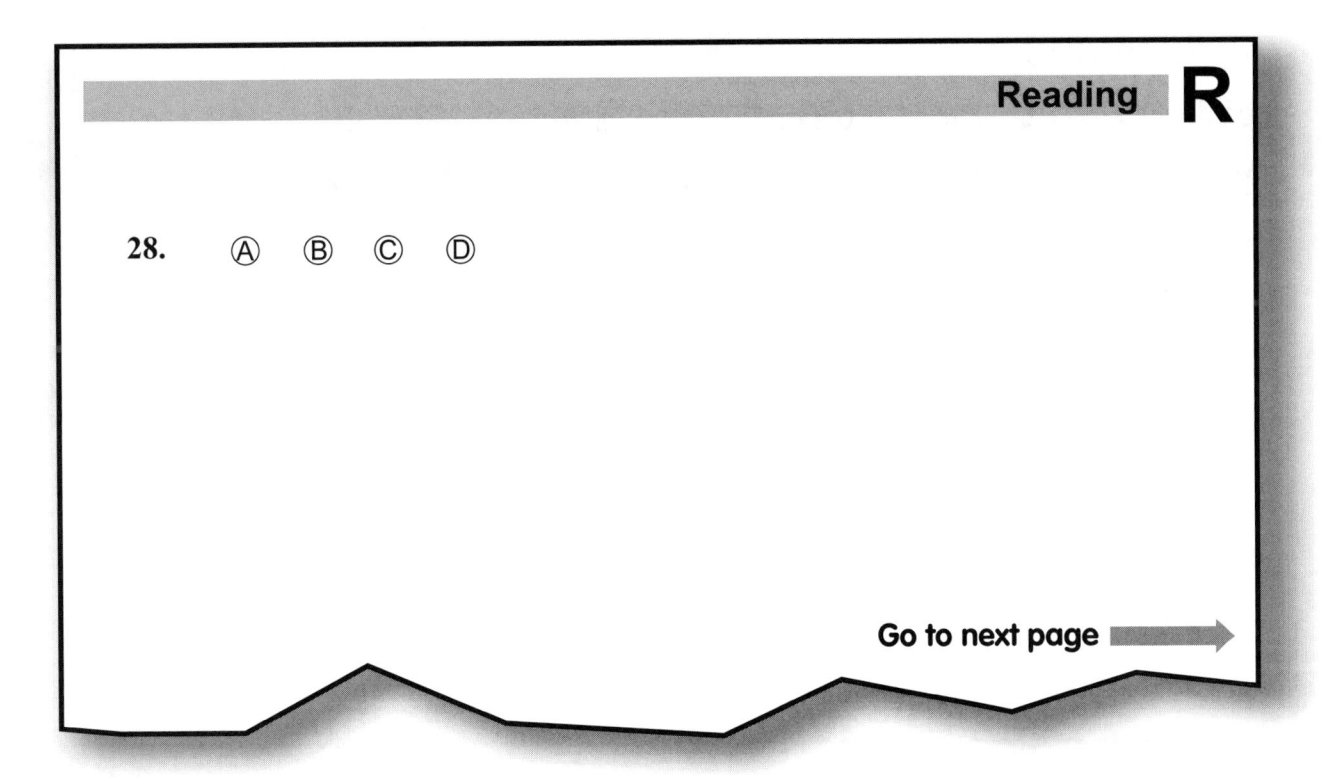

Analysis: The omniscient point of view is used when the reader knows about the internal thoughts of the characters in the story but does not say it out loud. The sentence given from the passage illustrates the omniscient point of view. Choice D is correct. First person and third person points of view are not used. Choices A and C are incorrect. There is no such term as second person. This is a distractor. Choice B is incorrect.

Question **29** *assesses:*

Reading Applications: Literary Text Standard

Benchmark D: Differentiate between the points of view in narrative text.

5. Identify recurring themes, patterns and symbols found in literature from different eras and cultures.

Reading R

29. This story takes place during the Civil War. How does the time period in which the story is set affect the theme?

   A. The mother says the girls don't deserve presents and is punishing them to teach them to obey her.

   B. The girls are not given presents to discourage them from joining the army, like their father.

   C. The girls are not given presents because they are so rich they can buy whatever they want for themselves.

   D. The mother wants the girls to focus on the suffering and sacrafices others are making because of the war instead of being selfish and focusing on what they want.

Go to next page

29. Ⓐ Ⓑ Ⓒ Ⓓ

Go to next page ➡

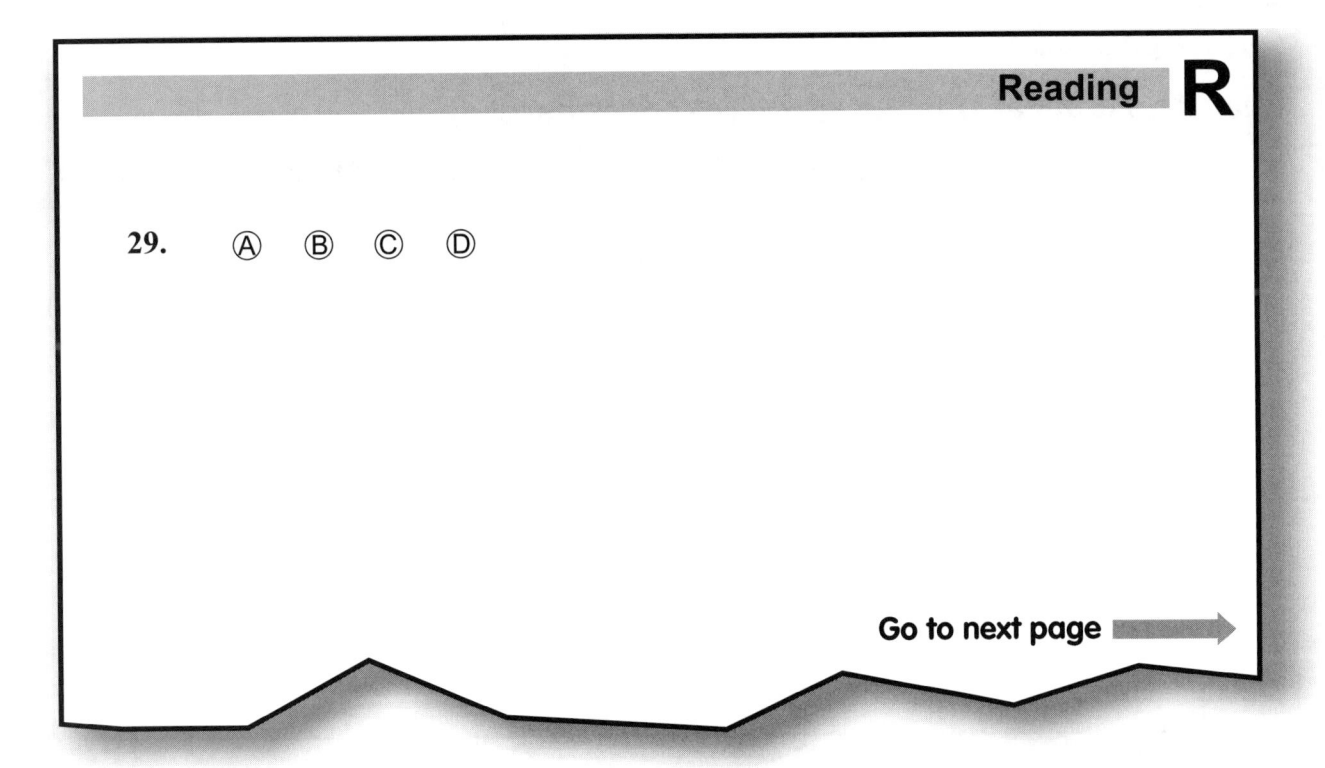

Analysis: *The story says, "You know the reason Mother proposed not having any presents this Christmas was because it is going to be a hard winter for everyone; and she thinks we ought not to spend money for pleasure, when our men are suffering so in the army." Choice D is correct. The text does not mention that the girls have misbehaved and are being punished. Choice A is incorrect. The text does not indicate that the girls have any interest in joining the army. Choice B is incorrect. The text says, "We've each got a dollar, and the army wouldn't be much helped by our giving that." Clearly, the girls aren't rich, but they decide to spend their money on small pleasures, like drawing pencils. Choice C is incorrect.*

Question **30** *assesses:*

Reading Applications: Literary Text Standard

Benchmark F: Identify similarities and differences of various literary forms and genres.

6. Explain the defining characteristics of literary forms and genres, including poetry, drama, myths, biographies, autobiographies, fiction, and non-fiction.

Reading R

30. The story that this selection came from was written to entertain the reader with an invented story. What genre best classifies this selection?

   A. non-fiction

   B. fiction

   C. poetry

   D. autobiography

Go to next page

30. Ⓐ Ⓑ Ⓒ Ⓓ

Go to next page ➡

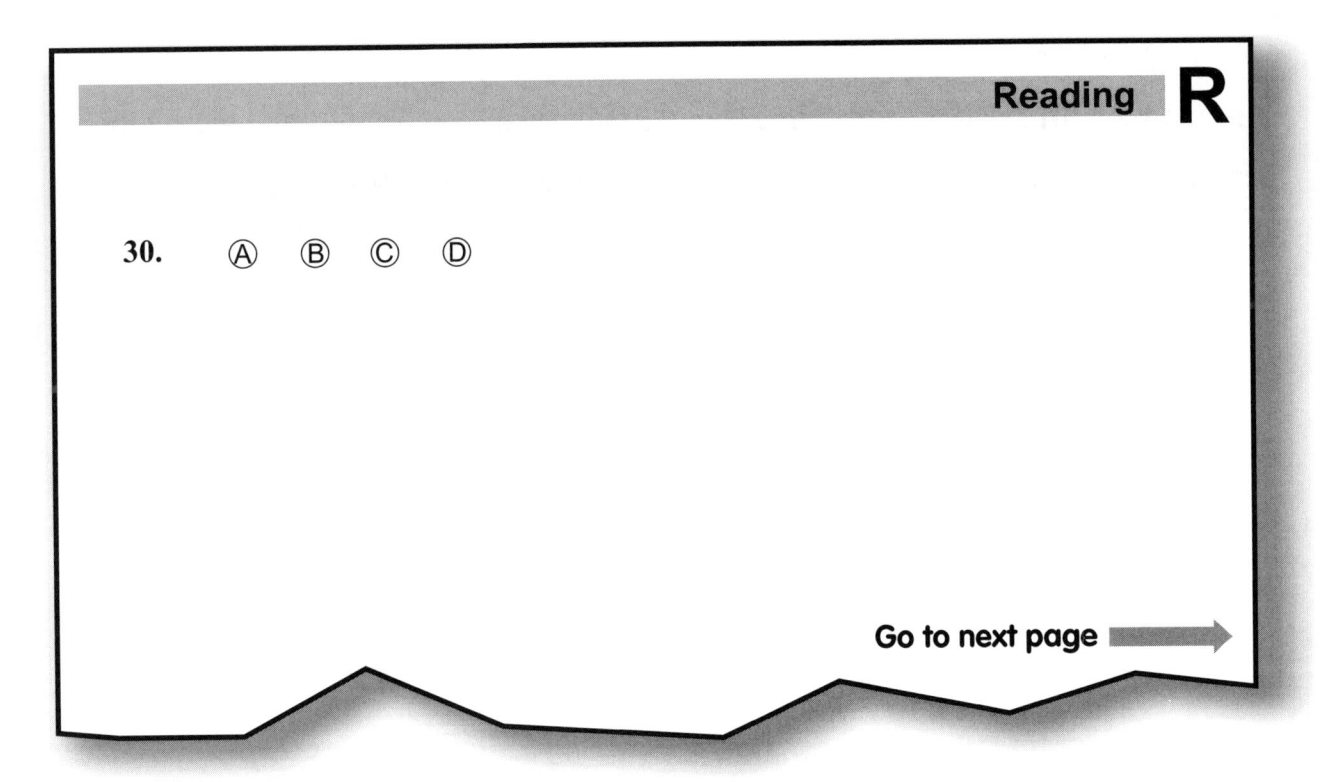

Analysis: *A story that is meant to entertain and is invented by the author is a fiction story. Choice B is correct. Choice A is incorrect because a non-fiction story states real facts, and is not invented. Choice C is incorrect. This selection does not use poetic devices. Choice D is incorrect since an autobiography is a true story about the author's life.*

Question **31** *assesses:*

Reading Applications: Literary Text Standard

Benchmark G: Explain how figurative language expresses ideas and conveys mood.

7. Distinguish how an author establishes mood and meaning through word choice, figurative language and syntax.

Reading R

31. " 'Christmas won't be Christmas without any presents,' **grumbled** Jo, lying on the rug."

    What mood does the author create by using the word **grumbled**?

    A. The author creates an angry mood by using the word *grumbled*.
    B. The author creates a sad mood by using the word *grumbled*.
    C. The author creates a happy mood by using the word *grumbled*.
    D. The author creates a nervous mood by using the word *grumbled*.

Show What You Know® on the OAT
Tutorial
Grade 6 Reading

31. Ⓐ Ⓑ Ⓒ Ⓓ

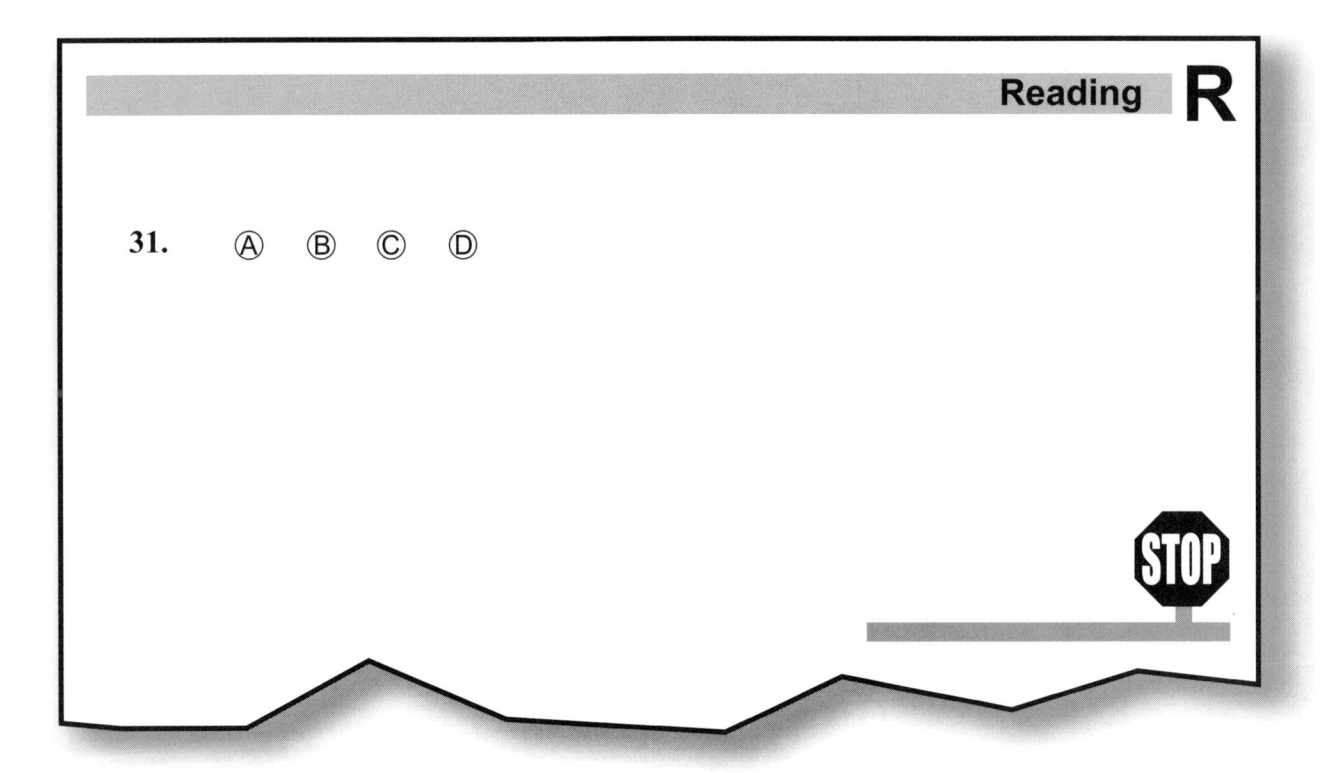

Analysis*: Jo grumbles these words to show that she is angry about not receiving any presents for Christmas. Choice A is correct. Choice B is incorrect because Jo is acting angry, not sad. Choice C is incorrect; Jo is angry, not happy. Choice D is incorrect because Jo is not nervous, she is angry.*

Reading Practice Test 1

Reading R

Directions:

Today you will be taking the Ohio Grade 6 Reading Practice Test. Three different types of questions appear on this test: multiple choice, short answer, and extended response.

There are several things to remember:

1. Read each question carefully. Think about what is being asked. Look carefully at graphs or diagrams because they help you understand the question.

2. For short-answer and extended-response questions, write your answers neatly and clearly in the space provided in the answer document. Any answers you write in the Student Test Booklet will not be scored.

3. Short-answer questions are worth two points. Extended-response questions are worth four points. Point values are printed near each question in your Student Test Booklet. The amount of space provided for your answers is the same for two- and four-point questions.

4. For multiple-choice questions, shade in the circle next to your choice in the answer document for the test question. Mark only one choice for each question. Darken completely the circles on the answer document. If you change an answer, make sure that you erase your old answer completely.

5. Do not spend too much time on one question. Go on to the next question and return to the question skipped after answering the remaining questions.

6. Check over your work when you are finished.

Go to next page

Reading

Stormy Nights

1. Hendrik still felt afraid of storms at night. If he awoke during a thunderstorm, fear seemed to take a grip on his throat until he could barely breathe.

2. Hendrik's bedroom looked ghostly when a storm shook the neighborhood. The room suddenly appeared white during flashes of lightning and then instantly grew darker-than-night during crashes of thunder. The flashes consisted of an unearthly light that shone in fits and starts: it turned on, then off, then on again. It made the room appear to move.

3. Imagine a bedroom rocking like a ship at sea! Hendrik would lie perfectly still under his warm, neat sheets, yet he felt as though he was drowning.

4. By the middle of June, there seemed to be a fresh storm every few nights. Often, the rain fell after midnight. By morning, things would look beautiful and damp. At dawn, the June grass lay like a smooth, green carpet glistening across the world. He tried to picture this at night, but the grass seemed different in darkness. After sunset, nothing looked green or smooth.

5. On the last night in June, Hendrik made himself comfortable on the old porch swing. He sat for a while. The night was completely dark, and it was impossible to see the dark grass. Silently, Hendrik watched and listened. He could hear life in the grass: thousands of crickets were communicating in the night. He thought about these little creatures that spend their entire lives outdoors, drinking the rainwater and the dew they discover on blades of grass. "It's amazing how those tiny insects survive all these turbulent storms," he thought. The sound of their chirping washed around him like gentle waves. The sound was comforting.

Use the selection to answer questions 1–6.

1. "The flashes consisted of an unearthly **light that shone in fits and starts.**"

   Which of the following best describes the meaning of the phrase **light that shone in fits and starts** in the sentence above?

   A. Hendrik thought he saw a flash of light, but it was only his imagination.
   B. The light appeared, then disappeared, then reappeared.
   C. The light disappeared.
   D. Hendrik enjoyed the light as it shined brightly through the night.

2. Read the dictionary meanings below for the word **grip**.

   > **grip** (grip) noun
   > **1.** a tight hold **2.** an intellectual understanding **3.** a mechanical device that holds something **4.** a suitcase

   "If he awoke during a thunderstorm, fear seemed to take a **grip** on his throat until he could barely breathe."

   Which meaning best fits the way **grip** is used in the sentence above?

   A. Meaning 1
   B. Meaning 2
   C. Meaning 3
   D. Meaning 4

3. "At dawn, the June grass lay like a smooth, green carpet **glistening** across the world."

   In the sentence above, what does **glistening** mean?

   A. giving a dull appearance
   B. giving a shiny appearance
   C. giving a green appearance
   D. giving a dry appearance

4. In paragraph 3, why is Hendrik lying perfectly still under his sheets?

   A. It is raining in his bedroom.
   B. His room appears to move and feels like a rocking ship.
   C. The trees outside are rocking like a ship.
   D. Hendrik is afraid to be alone.

Go to next page

Reading

5. "The sound of their chirping washed around him like gentle waves."

   In the context of this selection, this sentence means the sound of the crickets

   A. made Hendrik feel cleaner.

   B. covered Hendrik with water.

   C. created a flood in the area around Hendrik.

   D. seemed to float in the air around Hendrik.

6. How would this story be different if it were not storming outside?

   Write your answer in the **Answer Document**. (2 points)

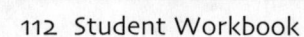

Reading

The New Scooter

1   A.J. tugged at the wrapping paper. Each tear revealed more of what he had hoped to see. Slowly, a brand new scooter made its way out of the box. A fresh-cut piece of chocolate cake sat untouched on the table. All A.J. could think about was trying out his new scooter. The raindrops tapping against the windowpane told him his first adventure would have to wait for another day.

2   The scooter may have been a birthday gift, but to A.J. it was much more than that. A.J. had asked for the same scooter for his last birthday; he had not gotten it. Instead, he had gotten some clothes and a speech from his parents about how important it was to do well in school. For the next year, A.J. worked as hard as he could in every class. He made the honor roll every quarter. A.J. looked at the scooter and smiled. To him, it stood for all the homework he had worked so hard on.

3   Another stormy day passed before A.J. saw light break through the dark clouds. The shiny scooter rested against the sun-porch railing. The fluorescent green wheels popped with color. The metallic shaft and handlebars glimmered in the light. A.J. grabbed his new toy and pushed both himself and the scooter outside with excitement. With one foot on the scooter's base, he used his other leg to give the scooter a gentle push. He then lifted his other leg to the scooter base and drifted down his driveway. There were several other kids outside enjoying the sun. It wasn't long before A.J. saw an old friend.

4   "Hey, Ann!" A.J. cried out. "What do you think of my new scooter?" He hardly gave her enough time to answer. He spun the scooter around on its front wheel, and he was off in another direction.

5   When Ann was able to get close to the duo, she admired A.J.'s new set of wheels. She had seen a scooter just like it at the bike shop, but the one she wanted had purple wheels. Ann watched as A.J. raced up and down the concrete driveway. It was as if he had been riding all his life.

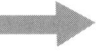

Reading

6   "You're pretty good at making that thing move," she said as he whizzed past her for the second time. A.J. stopped in front of Ann and decided this was the perfect opportunity to impress her with some tricks.

7   "Watch this!" A.J. said while he rode the scooter with just one hand. The more he rode, the braver he became. Holding onto the handlebars tightly, he made the scooter hop. Next, he lifted his right leg forward; then, he swung it behind him. He steered the scooter to the right and to the left, all while balancing on one leg. A.J. hardly let the scooter lose momentum before he would propel it forward again.

8   "Please be careful! You should be wearing a helmet if you're going to do tricks like that," Ann reminded him, but he didn't seem to pay attention to her.

9   It wasn't until A.J. felt like increasing the difficulty of his stunts that he actually let go of the scooter. He dropped it in the grass when he found some wooden boards lying by the side of the garage. He arranged them carefully until they formed a small ramp like the one he had seen in the bicycle magazines he kept in his room. "I'm ready for some action now," A.J. cried out, hoping Ann was watching him.

10   The first time over the ramp seemed easy, and A.J.'s confidence grew. "That was great!" Ann said, smiling.

11   She didn't want to admit it, but she hoped he would ask her if she wanted to ride his scooter. She wanted to try a trick or two, but A.J. wouldn't let go of his new scooter.

12   He wheeled the scooter around for his second attempt. "This one will be even better," he shouted.

13   A.J. zipped up and down the driveway and made his way toward the ramp. Just as the front wheel reached the board, the scooter flipped, leaving A.J. on the hard pavement. Ann rushed over and saw that A.J. had some scrapes and a large knot on his forehead. "Are you OK?" she said.

14   A.J. sat up slowly, rubbing his head. "On a scale of one to ten, what would you give me for that stunt?" asked A.J. It was his way of saying, "I'm fine." They both started laughing.

15   "I'll give you a ten if you promise not to do that again until you've got a helmet."

16   "It's a deal," said A.J. He climbed to his feet and looked around for the misplaced scooter. Upon careful examination, nothing seemed to be out of place. Although he knew he needed to take a break from the scooter, A.J. couldn't wait to try it again!

Use the selection to answer questions 7–16.

7. Which of the following offers the best description of A.J.?

   A. boring
   B. scared
   C. lonely
   D. adventurous

8. If the story were told from Ann's point of view, what would the story be titled?

   A. Someone Else's Ride
   B. My New Scooter
   C. My Scooter Adventure
   D. My Perfect Scooter

9. What problem does A.J. encounter in paragraph 1?

   A. A.J. wanted a scooter with purple wheels, but the scooter he receives has green wheels.
   B. A.J. can't use his new scooter because it is raining.
   C. A.J. doesn't like chocolate cake.
   D. A.J. can't use his new scooter because it is snowing.

10. "A.J. stopped in front of Ann and decided this was the perfect **opportunity** to impress her with some tricks."

    What does the word **opportunity** mean in the sentence above?

    A. to take a chance
    B. to be lucky
    C. a fit time
    D. an unfit time

11. How might the story change if A.J. were to decide not to increase the difficulty of his stunts?

    Write your answer in the **Answer Document**. (2 points)

12. Near the end of the selection, A.J. falls off his scooter. What does Ann say earlier in the selection that lets the reader know she is afraid this might happen?

    A. "That was great!"
    B. "You're pretty good at making that thing move."
    C. "You should wear a helmet if you're going to do tricks like that."
    D. "I'll give you a ten if you promise not to do that again until you've got a helmet."

Reading

13. What is A.J.'s new scooter a symbol of to him? Why did A.J. have to wait a year before getting his new scooter?

    Write your answer in the **Answer Document**. (4 points)

14. "The **fluorescent** green wheels popped with color."

    What is a synonym for the word **fluorescent** in the sentence above?

    A. dull
    B. glowing
    C. shiny
    D. cloudy

15. What happens toward the end of the story to make A.J. promise to wear a helmet?

    A. The scooter flips over leaving A.J. on the pavement.
    B. Ann wants to try to do tricks on the scooter.
    C. A.J. rides his scooter over the ramp and down the street.
    D. A.J. rides the scooter with just one hand, causing the scooter to flip over onto the pavement.

16. "Each tear **revealed** more of what he had hoped to see."

    What is an antonym for the word **revealed** in the sentence above?

    A. concealed
    B. exhibited
    C. showed
    D. displayed

Reading

An Island Paradise

1   What if you could visit a place that offers clear blue water, crystal beaches, and underwater adventures? Cozumel, in Mexico, is just such a place. Located off Mexico's Yucatan Peninsula, Cozumel has become a favorite vacation spot for divers and those who love the outdoors.

2   This exciting island is only 10 miles long and 28 miles wide, but it is Mexico's largest island. It attracts many visitors from across the globe each year. Most people travel to Cozumel to experience underwater diving at its best. It is thought of as one of the best diving spots in the world, second only to Australia.

3   Snorkeling is another activity Cozumel visitors enjoy. It is the second most popular water sport on the island. Beginners can snorkel right off the beaches of the hotels and see a variety of fish without going out too far. Another good place for beginning snorkelers is Chankanaab National Park. This park has shallow reefs that attract fish of all shapes, colors, and sizes.

4   If you're not interested in water sports, the Chankanaab Park also has nature trails where visitors can spend time walking and admiring the different plants of the island. You might even spot an iguana or two taking an afternoon nap in the sun!

5   San Miguel is the only town in Cozumel. Tourists from cruise ships and others who make the trip to town are in for a real treat. There are plenty of people who live in the town selling T-shirts, silver jewelry, and other goods made in Mexico.

6   It's easy to see why Cozumel is a favorite choice for outdoor adventures and sun-filled excitement!

Cozumel

7   Nestled between the trade routes to and from Honduras and Veracruz, Cozumel was well positioned as a seaport. Settled as early as 300 AD by the Maya, this island served many purposes. These purposes included being a pilgrimage site (a sacred place people journey to) and the center for Mayan trade.

8   As the Spanish arrived in the area in the late 1400s and early 1500s, the Mayans resisted a number of attempts at Spanish settlement. By 1519, however, a bitter struggle for the Yucatan Peninsula began. Slowly, the struggle crept outward. A Spanish presence began to take over the island. With the arrival of Hernan Cortéz and his men, many of the Mayan

Go to next page

R Reading

temples and shrines were destroyed. The foreigners also exposed the natives to smallpox. An epidemic (a very fast and wide spread of an illness) broke out, and by 1570, Cozumel's population declined to fewer than 300 people.

9   Throughout the 17th century, Cozumel was occupied mainly by pirates. The location of the island provided privacy and protection from danger. The area wasn't re-inhabited until 1848. At that time, Spanish settlers sought refuge from the Caste War, which was being fought on the mainland. A quiet fishing village was eventually established, and Cozumel remained as such until 1961. In that year, French explorer Jacques Cousteau declared the area's waters to be some of the most amazing for exploration. Since then, Cozumel has become a popular tourist destination, welcoming visitors from around the world every year.

Use the selections to answer questions 17–25.

17. How do the two selections differ in their approach to writing about Cozumel?

   A. "An Island Paradise" talks about the history of Cozumel; "Cozumel" talks about the island in the present.

   B. "An Island Paradise" talks about Cozumel in the present; "Cozumel" talks about the history of the island.

   C. "An Island Paradise" talks about Cozumel in the present; "Cozumel" talks about the future of the island.

   D. "An Island Paradise" talks about Cozumel in the future; "Cozumel" talks about the history of the island.

18. What is one similarity among the topics covered by the two selections?

   A. Both selections mention that San Miguel is a popular tourist destination.

   B. Both selections talk about pirates living on Cozumel.

   C. Both selections mention that Cozumel is a popular tourist destination.

   D. Both selections talk about Cozumel's nature trails.

19. Which of the following was an effect of foreigners exposing the natives of Cozumel to smallpox?

    A. Cozumel has become a popular tourist destination.

    B. Cozumel was well positioned as a seaport.

    C. Cozumel's population declined to fewer than 300 people.

    D. Many of the Mayan temples and shrines were destroyed.

20. Look at the outline of information below about the selection, "An Island Paradise."

    A. Facts about Cozumel
       1. Located off Mexico's Yucatan Peninsula
       2. 10 miles long and 28 miles wide

    B. Things to do in Cozumel
       1. Many travel there for underwater diving
       2. Many activities at Chankanaab National Park

    C. San Miguel
       1. _____
       2. People sell various Mexican-made items

    Which of these statements belongs in the blank under the heading "San Miguel"?

    A. The only town in Cozumel

    B. Shallow reefs that attract many types of fish

    C. Nature trails where people can walk and see plants

    D. Finest diving spot in the world

21. Look at the timeline below containing information from the selection, "Cozumel."

    ```
    Cozumel is settled by the Mayans.
              ↓
    Hernan Cortez arrives at Cozumel.
              ↓
    [                                ]
              ↓
    Spanish settlers seek refuge in Cozumel.
    ```

    Which event belongs in the empty box?

    A. A bitter struggle for the Yucatan Peninsula begins.

    B. Jacques Cousteau declares that Cozumel is a great place for underwater exploration.

    C. The Mayans first resist Spanish settlement of Cozumel.

    D. Cozumel is mainly occupied by pirates.

Reading

22. Snorkeling is a popular sport in Cozumel because

    A. snorkelers can see many fish without going very far from shore.
    B. Cozumel is considered the best snorkeling spot in the world.
    C. visitors can admire the many kinds of plants on the island.
    D. Cozumel is the largest island in Mexico.

23. "Cozumel was **occupied** mainly by pirates."

    What is the meaning of the word **occupied** in the sentence above?

    A. to do business with
    B. to take up space
    C. to take possession of
    D. to dwell or reside

24. Cozumel was occupied mainly by pirates throughout the 17th century because

    A. Cozumel was a fishing village.
    B. the island offfers snorkeling and shopping.
    C. the location of the island was a pilgrimage site and center for Mayan trade.
    D. the location of the island provided privacy and protection from danger.

25. "In that year, French explorer Jacques Cousteau declared the area's waters to be some of the most amazing for **exploration**."

    What does the word **exploration** mean in the sentence above?

    A. to establish
    B. to determine
    C. to declare
    D. to investigate

Reading

The Iditarod

1   Each year in March, Alaska is host to the Iditarod Trail Sled Dog Races, where drivers from around the world compete. In this contest, drivers (or "mushers") and their teams of dogs race from Anchorage, in south central Alaska, to Nome, on the west Bering Sea coast. The Iditarod is often called "The Last Great Race on Earth."

2   An Alaskan woman named Dorothy Page thought of the idea for the Iditarod. Page chaired a committee that was looking for projects to celebrate Alaska's centennial year (the year marking 100 years of being a state): 1967. She wanted to honor the mark sled-dog teams had made on Alaska's history. In the years before airplane travel was common and before snowmobiles were in use, dog teams were the main method of transportation during the winter months. Two short races were held along parts of the Iditarod Trail in 1967 and 1969, but the first full-length race wasn't held until 1973.

3   In addition to raising people's awareness of the effect of dog teams on Alaska's history, the Iditarod celebrates two important parts of Alaska's history. The first is to honor the heroism and the feats of the 1925 mushers who relayed medicine almost 700 miles to save sick residents in Nome. The Great Race also celebrates the Iditarod National Historic Trail, which was one of Alaska's major mail routes.

4   The Iditarod is a challenging race. The race covers roughly 1,150 miles across Alaska's sometimes harsh and dangerous wilderness. Some of the contributing factors involve the uncertain weather conditions of the Alaskan countryside and the difficult land. Mushers are likely to face blinding snowstorms and temperatures below zero. They may also face other factors such as dangerous wild animals and unsafe hills. It takes great willpower, strength, and courage to complete such a task. No one can ever be sure how long it will take the winner to cross the finish line, but the race usually lasts 10 to 17 days.

Reading

Use the selection to answer questions 26–31.

26. "The race covers roughly 1,150 miles across Alaska's sometimes **harsh** and dangerous wilderness."

    What does the word **harsh** mean in the sentence above?

    A. unknown
    B. rough
    C. hateful
    D. disagreeable

27. What would be a likely conclusion about a future Iditarod race?

    A. It will probably last longer than a week.
    B. It will probably last longer than a month.
    C. Mushers will probably face only good weather conditions.
    D. It will be an easy task for the mushers to complete.

28. List two reasons why the author believes the race takes up to 17 days to finish.

    Write your answer in the **Answer Document**. (2 points)

29. According to the selection, why is the Iditarod important to Alaskans?

    A. The Iditarod is a tribute to Dorothy Page, a woman who appreciated Alaska's history.
    B. The Iditarod is "The Last Great Race on Earth."
    C. Many tourists travel to Alaska to witness the Iditarod.
    D. The Iditarod honors a part of Alaska's history.

30. "The first is to honor the **heroism** and the feats of the 1925 mushers who relayed medicine almost 700 miles to save sick residents in Nome."

    What is a synonym for the word **heroism** in the sentence above?

    A. wimpiness
    B. fearfulness
    C. timidity
    D. bravery

31. What is the main reason the author wrote this selection?

    A. to inform readers about the importance and history of the Iditarod in Alaska
    B. to explain the history of the Iditarod National Trail
    C. to raise awareness of the dog teams that race in the Iditarod
    D. to entertain readers with heroic stories about Alaskan dog teams

Reading

The Professional

1   It was Marco's first job. The moment Mrs. Katz offered to pay him to take care of Savannah, he became a professional. He was only 12 years old.

2   Savannah, a large and beautiful female, already knew Marco. She ran out to meet him on the curb whenever he passed by her house. She always greeted him with his favorite sound: she sat down, she looked up at him, and she barked.

3   In February, a week after Marco's birthday, Mrs. Katz took a trip out of town. She left Savannah in the care of Marco Lombardy. His job was to stop by twice a day to feed and walk Savannah. Behind a tall basket on the porch, Mrs. Katz left her house key and Savannah's leather leash. The salary was great—four dollars per visit—and all Marco had to do was play with his favorite pet. Mrs. Katz even printed up a business card that included Marco's phone number and the title "Dog Sitter."

4   On Monday, the first day of the job, Marco awoke before dawn. In a flash, he put on warm clothing and pulled on snow boots. Cold air blew inside his collar as he rolled his bike out of the shed. A new layer of midnight snow covered the icy road.

5   "This is definitely the only bicycle on the street after a four-inch snow blizzard," he thought. At least the sidewalk had been cleared. He felt mature and responsible. No one else in the neighborhood seemed to be awake, yet he was already out of bed, dressed, and on his way to work.

6   Mrs. Katz's house was two blocks down the street. Her porch seemed to reach out over the top of the hill. When Marco let himself in at the back door, he found everything exactly where Mrs. Katz had said it would be. Running toward him from the silence of the empty house, Savannah gave him a three-minute hello. She was definitely glad to see him.

7   First, he tackled the kitchen duties. He cleaned out the water bowl, filled it with fresh water, and poured a scoop of dog food into Savannah's food bowl. One swipe with a paper towel was enough to give the floor a tidy appearance.

8   When he opened the kitchen door, Savannah leapt past him, out toward the snow. Marco held out the leash to show it was time for a walk. Savannah ran over obediently. Marco loved this part. She felt like his dog whenever he walked her on the leash.

9   Together, they trudged across the new snow. The morning seemed to shimmer and sparkle. Savannah's long, thin legs sank into deep snowdrifts with a crunchy-sounding step. When they reached Marco's house, at the bottom of the hillside, they turned to go back up the street. Slipping and sliding up the incline, the boy and the dog ran toward Mrs. Katz's house.

10   Marco's homemade chart rested on the kitchen table. He had carefully drawn a system for recording each visit and each feeding time. At the end of this first visit, he noted his time on the chart. For amusement, he also recorded Savannah's mood. This would be a fun feature of the job because Savannah was always in a good mood.

11   Before leaving, Marco stood proudly in Mrs. Katz's living room. Looking into the tall, elegant mirror, he smiled at the professional who was looking back at him.

Use the selection to answer questions 32–40.

32. Who is narrating this selection?

   A. Marco

   B. Savannah

   C. Mrs. Katz

   D. an unnamed narrator

33. At what point does Marco decide he is a professional?

   A. when Mrs. Katz makes a business card for him

   B. when Mrs. Katz offers to pay him for dogsitting

   C. when he rides his bike to Mrs. Katz house for the first time

   D. when he feeds Savannah for the first time

R Reading

34. Why does Marco create a chart, and what does he use this chart for?

    Write your answer in the **Answer Document**. (4 points)

35. The tone of paragraph 11 can best be described as

    A. gloomy.
    B. content.
    C. mysterious.
    D. nervous.

36. How does Marco feel about his job?

    Write your answer in the **Answer Document**. (2 points)

37. Which of the following does Marco do just for amusement?

    A. feed Savannah
    B. walk Savannah
    C. play with Savannah
    D. record Savannah's moods

38. Why are Marco and Savannah slipping and sliding up the street?

    A. The street is icy and cold.
    B. The street is dry and warm.
    C. The street is wet and muddy.
    D. It is raining outside.

39. Read the dictionary meanings below for the word **tackle.**

   > **tack•le** (tack´le) *verb*
   > **1.** to harness **2.** to take hold of
   > **3.** to undertake; to do **4.** to deal with

   "First, he **tackled** the kitchen duties."

   Which meaning best fits the way **tackled** is used in the sentence above?

   A. Meaning 1
   B. Meaning 2
   C. Meaning 3
   D. Meaning 4

40. "The morning seemed to shimmer and sparkle."

   Which of the following best describes the meaning of the sentence above?

   A. The sky looked shiny and bright.
   B. New snow made the morning appear to be bright and glisten.
   C. The sun was shining too bright.
   D. Marco was so happy that the morning sparkled.

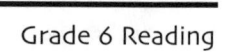

Reading

Use Pencil Please

1. Ⓐ Ⓑ Ⓒ Ⓓ
2. Ⓐ Ⓑ Ⓒ Ⓓ
3. Ⓐ Ⓑ Ⓒ Ⓓ
4. Ⓐ Ⓑ Ⓒ Ⓓ
5. Ⓐ Ⓑ Ⓒ Ⓓ

6. Write your response to question 6 in the space below.

Show What You Know® on the OAT
Grade 6 Reading

Practice Test 1
Answer Document

Reading R

7. Ⓐ Ⓑ Ⓒ Ⓓ

8. Ⓐ Ⓑ Ⓒ Ⓓ

9. Ⓐ Ⓑ Ⓒ Ⓓ

10. Ⓐ Ⓑ Ⓒ Ⓓ

11. Write your response to question 11 in the space below.

Go to next page

R Reading

12. Ⓐ Ⓑ Ⓒ Ⓓ

13. Write your response to question 13 in the space below.

_____

14. Ⓐ Ⓑ Ⓒ Ⓓ

15. Ⓐ Ⓑ Ⓒ Ⓓ

16. Ⓐ Ⓑ Ⓒ Ⓓ

17. Ⓐ Ⓑ Ⓒ Ⓓ

18. Ⓐ Ⓑ Ⓒ Ⓓ

Go to next page ➡

Reading

19. Ⓐ Ⓑ Ⓒ Ⓓ

20. Ⓐ Ⓑ Ⓒ Ⓓ

21. Ⓐ Ⓑ Ⓒ Ⓓ

22. Ⓐ Ⓑ Ⓒ Ⓓ

23. Ⓐ Ⓑ Ⓒ Ⓓ

24. Ⓐ Ⓑ Ⓒ Ⓓ

25. Ⓐ Ⓑ Ⓒ Ⓓ

26. Ⓐ Ⓑ Ⓒ Ⓓ

27. Ⓐ Ⓑ Ⓒ Ⓓ

R Reading

28. Write your response to question 28 in the space below.

_____
_____
_____
_____
_____
_____
_____
_____
_____
_____
_____
_____
_____
_____
_____
_____

29. Ⓐ Ⓑ Ⓒ Ⓓ

30. Ⓐ Ⓑ Ⓒ Ⓓ

31. Ⓐ Ⓑ Ⓒ Ⓓ

32. Ⓐ Ⓑ Ⓒ Ⓓ

33. Ⓐ Ⓑ Ⓒ Ⓓ

Go to next page ➡

34. Write your response to question 34 in the space below.

[lined response box]

35. Ⓐ Ⓑ Ⓒ Ⓓ

R Reading

36. Write your response to question 36 in the space below.

[lined response space]

37. Ⓐ Ⓑ Ⓒ Ⓓ

38. Ⓐ Ⓑ Ⓒ Ⓓ

39. Ⓐ Ⓑ Ⓒ Ⓓ

40. Ⓐ Ⓑ Ⓒ Ⓓ

Reading Practice Test 2

Reading R

Directions:

Today you will be taking the Ohio Grade 6 Reading Practice Test. Three different types of questions appear on this test: multiple choice, short answer, and extended response.

There are several things to remember:

1. Read each question carefully. Think about what is being asked. Look carefully at graphs or diagrams because they help you understand the question.

2. For short-answer and extended-response questions, write your answers neatly and clearly in the space provided in the answer document. Any answers you write in the Student Test Booklet will not be scored.

3. Short-answer questions are worth two points. Extended-response questions are worth four points. Point values are printed near each question in your Student Test Booklet. The amount of space provided for your answers is the same for two- and four-point questions.

4. For multiple-choice questions, shade in the circle next to your choice in the answer document for the test question. Mark only one choice for each question. Darken completely the circles on the answer document. If you change an answer, make sure that you erase your old answer completely.

5. Do not spend too much time on one question. Go on to the next question and return to the question skipped after answering the remaining questions.

6. Check over your work when you are finished.

Go to next page

Reading

Our National Bird

1   The bald eagle was chosen as the national symbol of the United States in 1782. It was chosen because of its long life, great strength, and majestic looks. At that time, people also believed that the bald eagle existed only in the area known as the United States. The eagle became a national emblem with the adoption of the Great Seal of the United States. The bald eagle serves as a sign of greatness and represents freedom. You can see the eagle on some U.S. coins, such as the quarter, the silver dollar, and the half dollar.

2   Eagles are large and beautiful birds with long, broad wingspans—from 70–90 inches. This helps them soar high in the air. Adult eagles have blackish-brown feathers on their bodies and white heads, necks, and tails. Some believe the white feathers on the eagle's head give it the appearance of being bald. At one time the word "bald" meant "white." However, the eagle really isn't bald or featherless at all.

3   Eagles are at the top of the food chain and have very few enemies. The eagle's powerful beak can tear through the prey it catches with its strong legs and talons. A part of the sea fish eagle group, these birds will eat both freshwater and saltwater fish. Eagles are known for their excellent eyesight and are able to see fish in the water from several hundred feet above. When they see a fish in the water, they will swoop down and catch it with their sharp talons or claws. Although they are mainly fish eaters, they will also feast on other available food sources, including dead animals. This fact adds to the eagle's reputation as a scavenger.

4   In the wild, eagles can live to be twenty or thirty years old. They are found in most of North America, ranging from Alaska and Canada to northern Mexico. The bald eagle was put on the endangered species list in 1967, because the birds were dying out. The birds have since made a reappearance, however. Today, there are about 50,000 bald eagles in the United States, and they are no longer considered an endangered species.

The Great Seal

5   The Great Seal of the United States shows a wide-spread bald eagle. On the eagle's breast, a shield appears. The shield contains thirteen parallel red and white stripes. Also present is a blue field with 13 stars. In the eagle's right talon, there is an olive branch. The left talon carries a bundle of thirteen arrows. In the eagle's beak, the bird carries a scroll inscribed with the motto *e pluribus unum*, which translates as "one out of many."

Go to next page

Use the selections to answer questions 1–9.

1. Which of the following explains how the bald eagle received its name?

    A. The head of the bald eagle is featherless, but the rest of the bird has feathers.

    B. The word "bald" once meant "white," and the bald eagle has white feathers on its head.

    C. The bald eagle is a featherless bird.

    D. The word "white" once meant "bald," and the bald eagle's head is featherless.

2. Which of the following does not represent a reason why the bald eagle was chosen as a national symbol for the United States?

    A. At the time the bird was chosen, people believed the bald eagle could only be found in the United States.

    B. The bald eagle has great strength.

    C. The bald eagle is actually bald; at one time, the word "bald" meant "white."

    D. The bald eagle has a long life span.

3. Name two things that are referred to in both selections.

    Write your answer in the **Answer Document**. (2 points)

4. If the bald eagle had not been placed on the Great Seal of the United States, then

    A. it probably would not exist outside of the United States.

    B. it probably would be pictured on all United States coins.

    C. it probably would not have become a national emblem.

    D. it probably would not have a reputation as a scavenger.

5. What is the author's purpose for writing the selection, "Our National Bird"?

    A. The author wants to entertain readers with stories about eagles.

    B. The author wants to inform readers about the importance of the bald eagle.

    C. The author wants to persuade readers to become involved with endangered species groups.

    D. The author wants to describe to readers what the Great Seal of the United States looks like.

R Reading

6. According to the reading selection, "Our National Bird," what do eagles prey on? What makes it easy for the eagle to prey on these food sources?

   Write your answer in the **Answer Document**. (4 points)

7. Which of the following is an effect of the bald eagle becoming designated as an endangered species?

   A. "In the wild, eagles can live to be twenty or thirty years old."

   B. "Today, there are about 50,000 bald eagles in the United States, and they are no longer considered and endangered species."

   C. "Eagles are on the top of the food chain and have very few enemies."

   D. "The eagle became a national emblem with the adoption of the Great Seal of the United States."

8. "In the eagle's beak, the bird carries a **scroll** inscribed with the motto *e pluribus unum*, which translates as 'one out of many.'"

   What does the word **scroll** mean in the sentence above?

   A. a roll of parchment paper with writing on it

   B. an ancient book

   C. a list of names

   D. to unroll

9. "It was chosen because of its long life, great strength, and **majestic** looks."

   What is a synonym for the word **majestic** in the sentence above?

   A. unrefined

   B. humble

   C. custom

   D. grand

Pep Rally Return!
By Meredith T.

1   My fellow students, I say it is time for a Valencia School pep rally! We haven't seen one of these events in three years, and Valencia School pride has suffered.

2   According to Principal Barrett, pep rallies were called off after a student trick. He wouldn't give many details, but he did say the trickster is no longer a Valencia student. To prevent future incidents, Mr. Barrett banned these important events that build school spirit. Until now, a school year without pep rallies has never been questioned.

3   I would like all Valencia students to support my request for a Valencia School pep rally. When I think back to the last rally I attended, I remember the excitement that buzzed through the halls. We all dressed in our Valencia School colors: purple and gold. Even my teacher at the time, Miss Burke, was excited. She wore a purple wig. We crowded into the gym as the band played the Valencia School song. We shook purple flags and chanted cheers. I felt as though Valencia School was the best school in the whole world.

4   Next month, Valencia School is hosting a basketball tournament. We want the visiting schools to see what a great place Valencia School is. We also want our team to know the school is behind them all the way. We could fill the gym with signs of encouragement and purple and gold streamers. School pride would be spilling not only from every wall but also from every student's face.

5   A pep rally would give band members a chance to demonstrate their talents. Our cheerleaders could teach new students Valencia School chants. The basketball team would know the school supports them; an improved sense of pride would help the team do well in the tournament.

6   Valencia School is a great place to be. If you agree with this statement, you must agree that a pep rally celebrating Valencia School pride is an important custom to be revived. The next time you see Principal Barrett, tell him, "It's time for a pep rally return!"

Reading

A Letter from Principal Barrett

7   Dear Valencia School Students,

8   Recently, many of you have been asking why we no longer have pep rallies. Pep rallies at this school were officially cancelled after one student played a trick during a pep rally. In general, very few students were well-behaved during pep rallies.

9   The purpose of a pep rally is to get students excited about something important going on at the school. Instead, many students used a pep rally as a chance to talk to their friends. During one of the last pep rallies held at this school, the cheerleaders, the band, and the basketball team were all working very hard to get students excited. At first, it seemed to work—students chanted and cheered, and a buzz of excitement filled the gym. But after a few minutes, when I looked around, I didn't see students being supportive. I saw students talking, giggling with friends, and passing notes. There were even some students who were making fun of those who were out on the gym's floor.

10 I would love to be able to hold pep rallies here at Valencia School. First, students are going to have to convince me that they want pep rallies for the right reasons. If you can make me believe this is the real reason you want to have pep rallies, then maybe we can give this tradition another try.

11 Sincerely,
    Principal Barrett

Use the selection to answer questions 10–18.

10. What incident occurred to cause Principal Barrett to permanently cancel pep rallies?

    A. Students showed too much school pride during rallies.

    B. A student played a trick during a pep rally.

    C. Students were talking and giggling with friends during the rallies.

    D. A student passed a note to Principal Barrett during a pep rally.

11. How are the two authors' perspectives different?

    Write your answer in the **Answer Document**. (2 points)

12. Principal Barrett wrote a letter to the Valencia School students because

   A. he wanted to tell the story of the school's last pep rally.

   B. he wanted to persuade students to hold more pep rallies.

   C. he wanted to inform students about pep rallies at other schools.

   D. he wanted to explain his reasons for not having pep rallies.

13. What is the purpose of the selection "Pep Rally Return!"?

   A. to persuade students to cancel pep rallies.

   B. to persuade students to convince Principal Barrett to reinstate pep rallies

   C. to persuade Principal Barrett to cancel school pep rallies

   D. to persuade Miss Burke to reinstate school pep rallies

14. The authors of the two selections are similar in that

   A. they both would like the school to be able to have pep rallies again.

   B. they both think students see pep rallies mainly as a time to talk to friends.

   C. they both think school pride has suffered without pep rallies.

   D. they both would like to have the pep rallies cancelled permanently.

15. Which of the following statements would Meredith T. most likely include in her writing?

   A. Students will lose valuable learning time in the classroom if they attend a pep rally.

   B. New students don't want to learn school chants.

   C. Students will be tempted to pull tricks if a school pep rally is held.

   D. School pep rallies help students appreciate their school.

Reading

16. "Even my teacher at the time, Miss Burke, was excited; she wore a purple wig."

    Why does the author choose to include this information?

    A. She wants readers to understand how Miss Burke feels about pep rallies.
    B. She wants readers to know that teachers appreciate pep rallies, too.
    C. She wants readers to know that Miss Burke is a fun teacher.
    D. She wants readers to know that purple is one of the school colors.

17. "If you agree with this statement, you must agree that a pep rally celebrating Valencia School pride is an important custom to be **revived**."

    What is an antonym for the word **revived** from the sentence above?

    A. recovered
    B. activated
    C. stimulated
    D. inhibited

18. Which of the following best describes the meaning of the phrase "excitement that buzzed through the halls"?

    A. The hall was actually making a buzzing sound.
    B. The hall was vibrating.
    C. The students were so happy about the pep rally that they talked about the rally in the hallway.
    D. The students were so happy about the pep rally that they walked quietly through the halls.

Storm Chasers

1. Many people fear "Mother Nature" and the unpredictable weather she has been known to cause, but there are those who are fascinated by her. They want to see her effects up close. As a matter of fact, they go out looking for bad weather and storms. These people are known as storm chasers.

2. Storm chasers are everyday people who are awestruck by severe storms and extreme weather. They actually go out in search of it! They sometimes travel hundreds of miles from state to state in search of the big storm. Certain areas of the United States, including the Great Plains and the Midwest, are known to produce such storms. As a result, many storm chasers come from those areas or settle there.

3. Usually, the main goal of the storm chaser is to witness a tornado, but this isn't always the case. Oftentimes, the severe weather becomes dangerous. The storm chasers could be risking their own safety if they continue to chase the storm. When the risk is too great, storm chasers have to give up the chase. For most, however, the real reward is the total experience of the storm itself and getting to see nature's awesome power up close.

4. Technological advances have given meteorologists, scientists who study weather, the ability to predict certain weather patterns and storms. Meteorologists are people who have earned a special degree from a university and who work to forecast and report the weather.

5. Today, storm chasers have many more tools and information to work with than the first chasers did. Using this information, storm chasers are likely to experience more storms than ever before. While most storm chasers are there for the experience and to take photographs or to shoot video, some do collect meteorological information for weather research.

6. Storm chasers come from all walks of life, but their interest in weather and storms gives them something in common. As long as there is weather to observe, storm chasers will continue to follow the skies.

Reading

Use the selection to answer questions 19–24.

19. According to paragraph 3, what is the real reward for storm chasers?

    Write your answer in the **Answer Document**. (2 points)

20. Which of the following is supported by details from the selection?

    A. Storm chaser is another name for a meteorologist.
    B. Storm chasing is more advanced today than it was before.
    C. Storm chasers train in college.
    D. Storm chasing is no longer possible.

21. "Meteorologists are people who have earned a special degree from a university and who work to **forecast** and report the weather."

    What does the word **forecast** mean in the sentence above?

    A. to predict
    B. to gather
    C. to doubt
    D. to surprise

22. Meteorologists and storm chasers are similar because

    A. they both receive degrees from universities.
    B. they are both interested in weather.
    C. they both travel to find storms.
    D. they are both from the Midwest.

23. "Many people fear 'Mother Nature' and the **unpredictable** weather she has been known to cause, but there are those who are fascinated by her."

    What does **unpredictable** mean in the sentence above?

    A. not expected
    B. expected
    C. safe
    D. stormy

24. According to the selection, what causes storm chasers to seek out severe weather?

    A. They are paid by the government to do weather research.
    B. Meteorologists ask the storm chasers to do weather research.
    C. Storm chasers want to obtain storm-chasing licenses.
    D. Storm chasers are fascinated by severe weather and want to experience it firsthand.

The Exchange Student

1   "When does her plane arrive?" Emily asked her mother impatiently. Emily wasn't very good at hiding her excitement. She knew her mother did not want to hear her say one more word, but Emily didn't care.

2   "For the last time, we'll leave for the airport around two o'clock. Misa's flight doesn't get in until three this afternoon," replied Mrs. Norris, who was obviously annoyed by her daughter's repeated questioning. "I know you're excited, but this is Misa's first time in the United States. We want to make her feel right at home here in New York," Emily's mother reminded her.

3   The Norris family had agreed to host a foreign exchange student for the summer. The International Student Exchange, a program sponsored by Emily's school, had invited students from around the world to enjoy two months in New York. Emily had been waiting for the exchange student to arrive ever since. Today, the waiting would be over. Misa was traveling from Italy on Flight 223 out of Milan to America.

4   Mrs. Norris had prepared the extra bedroom for Misa. It was a few steps down the hall from Emily's room. Emily gave the room one last glance as two o'clock approached. She wanted to make sure everything was in order for Misa's arrival.

5   Emily and her mother reached the airport. They found a flight schedule posted on an electronic display board. As Mrs. Norris searched for Misa's flight, a voice on the airport speaker announced that Flight 223 from Italy had landed. Emily's stomach filled with butterflies. The moment she had been waiting for had finally arrived. Several transatlantic passengers, looking tired and anxious, walked past. Emily looked around each person, trying to spot Misa.

7   "I think I see her! I think I see her!" Emily said as she tugged on her mom's arm.

8   "Hello, Misa!" Emily waved. "Welcome to the United States!" The girls gave each other hugs. Misa asked question after question, while Emily answered question after question. Mrs. Norris smiled. "At least Misa has as many questions as Emily," she thought to herself.

AIRLINE FLIGHT NO.	DEPARTURE CITY	ARRIVAL TIME	STATUS
International 456	London	2:45 p.m.	On time
French Air 701	Paris	3:15 p.m.	On time
Fly Away 313	Houston	4:05 p.m.	Delayed
Continuous 223	Milan	3:00 p.m.	On time
Air Ways 725	Washington	5:25 p.m.	On time
King Jet 687	Berlin	2:30 p.m.	Delayed

Go to next page

Reading

Use the selection to answer questions 25–30.

25. Emily was excited because

   A. she wanted to meet Misa.
   B. she wanted to fly on an airplane.
   C. she wanted to go to the airport.
   D. she wanted to visit Misa in Italy.

26. Using the Airline Flight chart, which airline flight number was scheduled to land first?

   A. Flight 725
   B. Flight 456
   C. Flight 687
   D. Flight 223

27. What will Emily most likely do when she and Misa get home?

   A. Emily will ignore Misa.
   B. Emily will show Misa around the house.
   C. Emily will become angry with Misa for asking so many questions.
   D. Emily will do her homework.

28. "Several **transatlantic passengers**, looking tired and anxious, walked past."

   What does **transatlantic passengers** mean in the sentence above?

   Write your answer in the **Answer Document**. (2 points)

29. How might the story change if it were told from Misa's point of view?

   A. The story would not be about an exchange student.
   B. Misa would talk about how unhappy she was to be traveling to America.
   C. Misa would explain what her plane trip from Milan was like.
   D. Misa would tell about the room in her house that she will share with Emily.

30. Which of the following is a good summary of paragraph 4?

   A. The Norris family prepared a special bedroom for their exchange student, and Emily wanted to make sure their guest felt welcome.
   B. Emily made sure everything was in order.
   C. Emily cleaned Misa's bedroom before meeting Misa at the airport because the room was dirty.
   D. The Norris family divided Emily's room into two sections, so that each girl would have her own space.

Chewing Gum

1   Did you know that the discovery of chewing gum might date back to 50 AD when ancient people chewed the resin from trunks of trees? Historians have found that the Greeks chewed tree resin from the mastic tree. They called this early chewing gum "mastiche." Back then, gum was thought to clean teeth and to freshen breath. The Greeks weren't the only ones to chew the resin substance, though. Throughout Central America, the Mayan people chewed sap from the sapodilla tree; they called this sap "chicle." Also, North American Indians were known to chew the sap from spruce trees.

2   It wasn't until 1848 that the first gum was manufactured and sold to the public. John Curtis and his brother produced spruce gum, which they called "State of Maine Pure Spruce Gum." Sales were slow. It wasn't until a more popular type of gum came to be that the Curtis brothers found success with their idea. In 1850, they added paraffin gum to their product line. The paraffin gum had a better texture than the spruce gum, and it could be produced in a variety of flavors. The improvements satisfied people's tastes, and the public began to buy more gum.

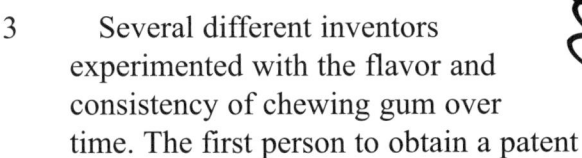

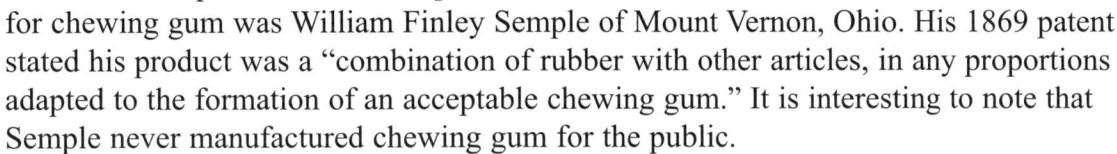

3   Several different inventors experimented with the flavor and consistency of chewing gum over time. The first person to obtain a patent for chewing gum was William Finley Semple of Mount Vernon, Ohio. His 1869 patent stated his product was a "combination of rubber with other articles, in any proportions adapted to the formation of an acceptable chewing gum." It is interesting to note that Semple never manufactured chewing gum for the public.

4   During the late 1860s, one-time president of Mexico Antonio Lopez de Santa Anna settled in New Jersey. Santa Anna brought a large amount of Mexican chicle to the United States. He hoped he would be able to sell it. He met Thomas Adams of Staten, New York, and discussed the idea of using the chicle to invent a rubber-like substance that could be used to make carriage tires. Adams had been working as a photographer, but he also dabbled in many other trades. The idea of the new invention interested Adams, so he agreed to buy Santa Anna's chicle supply.

5   Adams experimented with the chicle, but each time he was disappointed with his results. In fact, he almost threw away the entire supply. By accident, an idea sparked in Adams: he would use the chicle to create a chewing gum. His development was successful, and Adams was soon selling chewing gum in many local stores. By 1871, Adams had

Reading

developed and patented a gum-producing machine. Once sold in lumps or chunks, Adams' gum now sold in sticks. His first flavored gum was made with licorice flavoring. He called this type of gum "Black Jack." In some parts of the country, this brand can still be found. Another of Adams' chewing gums, Tutti-Frutti, became the first chewing gum to be sold in a New York City subway station vending machine.

6   While Adams was able to give his gums some flavor, their tastiness was often lost after just a few moments of chewing. Around 1880, John Colgan of Louisville, Kentucky, had an idea for how to extend gum's flavor. He added flavoring to the sugar before the sugar was added to the chicle. This way, the gum's flavoring lasted longer. Colgan's Taffy Tolu Chewing Gum was a quick success.

Bubble Gum

7   It wasn't until shortly after the turn of the century that bubble gum came to be. In 1906, Frank Fleer, of the Fleer Company, invented a form of bubble gum named "Blibber-Blubber." Unfortunately, this bubble gum was so sticky it never made it to store shelves. It wasn't until many years later that Walter Diemer, an accountant for Fleer's chewing gum company, created a new bubble gum while experimenting with different recipes for fun. What he developed was gum that was not as sticky and that seemed to stretch more than the regular chewing gum. This stretching characteristic was perfect for blowing bubble gum bubbles. Diemer's gum was colored pink because it was the only color the Fleer Company had on hand at the time. Diemer thought the pink color made his bubble gum more appealing to the eye, and to this day, most bubble gum is pink.

8   Over the past century, the popularity of bubble gum has grown and grown. Stores now sell bubble gum in all shapes, sizes, and flavors. Gum comes in shredded pieces, in long strips rolled like tape, and in squeezable tubes. Popular flavors include watermelon, mint, cotton candy, and cherry, just to name a few. Next time you're in the mood for some gum, you may face a selection of more than 30 different varieties. Each time you chew on a piece of gum, just think, you're enjoying something that has developed and changed over the past 2,000 years. Who knows what the future of gum will bring!

Use the selection to answer questions 31–40.

31. What are the differences between chewing gum and bubble gum?

    Write your answer in the **Answer Document**. (4 points)

32. What is the main idea of paragraph 1 of "Chewing Gum"?

    A. Some natural forms of gum, which were used for many purposes, have been around for centuries.

    B. The earliest chewing gum on record is "mastiche," which was enjoyed by the Greeks.

    C. The Mayan people were the first to discover "chicle."

    D. North American Indians chewed sap from spruce trees.

33. Paragraphs 4 and 5 of "Chewing Gum" are organized by

    A. giving the causes and effects of Adams' experiments with chicle.

    B. comparing and contrasting different ways to make gum.

    C. describing all the problems Adams had while working with chicle.

    D. explaining the sequence of how chicle is formed into gum.

34. Which of the following sentences explain why Blibber Blubber never became as popular as Bubble Gum?

    A. "It wasn't until shortly after the turn of the century that bubble gum came to be."

    B. "Diemer's gum was colored pink because it was the only color the Fleer Company had on hand at the time."

    C. "In 1906, Frank Fleer, of the Fleer Company, invented a form of bubble gum named 'Blibber-Blubber.'"

    D. "Unfortunately, this bubble gum was so sticky it never made it to store shelves."

35. According to the passage "Chewing Gum," which of these events occurred first?

    A. Inventor Thomas Adams invented a gum machine.

    B. John Curtis and his brother produced spruce gum.

    C. Paraffin gum was introduced to the public.

    D. John Colgan added sugar to gum.

R Reading

36. "Several different inventors experimented with the flavor and **consistency** of chewing gum over time."

    What is the meaning of the word **consistency** in the sentence above?

    A. firmness
    B. reliable
    C. compatible
    D. temperature

37. Which sentence from the passage "Chewing Gum" supports the idea that creating paraffin gum was an important step for the Curtis brothers?

    A. "It wasn't until 1848 that the first gum was manufactured and sold to the public."
    B. "John Curtis and his brother produced spruce gum, which they called 'State of Maine Pure Spruce Gum.'"
    C. "The improvements satisfied people's tastes, and the public began to buy more gum."
    D. "In 1850, they added paraffin gum to their product line."

38. In what year was gum first manufactured and sold to the public?

    A. 1848
    B. 1850
    C. 1869
    D. 1871

39. Which sentence explains how John Colgan extended the flavoring in gum?

    A. "By 1871, Adams had developed and patented a gum producing machine."
    B. "Once sold in lumps or chunks, Adams' gum now sold in sticks."
    C. "By accident, an idea sparked in Adams he would use the chicle to create chewing gum."
    D. "He added flavoring to the sugar before the sugar was added to the chicle."

40. "Next time you're in the mood for some gum, you may face a selection of more than 30 different **varieties**."

    What is the meaning of the word **varieties** in the sentence above?

    A. unusual
    B. changes
    C. collections
    D. assortments

STOP

Show What You Know® on the OAT

Grade 6 Reading

Practice Test 2
Answer Document

Reading R

1. Ⓐ Ⓑ Ⓒ Ⓓ

2. Ⓐ Ⓑ Ⓒ Ⓓ

3. Write your response to question 3 in the space below.

_____
_____
_____
_____
_____
_____
_____
_____
_____
_____
_____
_____
_____

Go to next page

Practice Test 2
Answer Document

R Reading

4. Ⓐ Ⓑ Ⓒ Ⓓ

5. Ⓐ Ⓑ Ⓒ Ⓓ

6. Write your response to question 6 in the space below.

_____
_____
_____
_____
_____
_____
_____
_____
_____
_____
_____
_____
_____
_____
_____

7. Ⓐ Ⓑ Ⓒ Ⓓ

8. Ⓐ Ⓑ Ⓒ Ⓓ

9. Ⓐ Ⓑ Ⓒ Ⓓ

10. Ⓐ Ⓑ Ⓒ Ⓓ

Go to next page

Reading

11. Write your response to question 11 in the space below.

[lined response box]

12. Ⓐ Ⓑ Ⓒ Ⓓ

13. Ⓐ Ⓑ Ⓒ Ⓓ

14. Ⓐ Ⓑ Ⓒ Ⓓ

15. Ⓐ Ⓑ Ⓒ Ⓓ

16. Ⓐ Ⓑ Ⓒ Ⓓ

17. Ⓐ Ⓑ Ⓒ Ⓓ

Practice Test 2
Answer Document

R Reading

18. Ⓐ Ⓑ Ⓒ Ⓓ

19. Write your response to question 19 in the space below.

_____

20. Ⓐ Ⓑ Ⓒ Ⓓ
21. Ⓐ Ⓑ Ⓒ Ⓓ
22. Ⓐ Ⓑ Ⓒ Ⓓ
23. Ⓐ Ⓑ Ⓒ Ⓓ
24. Ⓐ Ⓑ Ⓒ Ⓓ

Go to next page

Show What You Know® on the OAT
Grade 6 Reading

Practice Test 2
Answer Document

Reading R

25. Ⓐ Ⓑ Ⓒ Ⓓ

26. Ⓐ Ⓑ Ⓒ Ⓓ

27. Ⓐ Ⓑ Ⓒ Ⓓ

28. Write your response to question 28 in the space below.

_____

29. Ⓐ Ⓑ Ⓒ Ⓓ

30. Ⓐ Ⓑ Ⓒ Ⓓ

Go to next page

R Reading

31. Write your response to question 31 in the space below.

[lined response space]

32. Ⓐ Ⓑ Ⓒ Ⓓ

33. Ⓐ Ⓑ Ⓒ Ⓓ

34. Ⓐ Ⓑ Ⓒ Ⓓ

35. Ⓐ Ⓑ Ⓒ Ⓓ

36. Ⓐ Ⓑ Ⓒ Ⓓ

37. Ⓐ Ⓑ Ⓒ Ⓓ

Go to next page

Reading

38. Ⓐ Ⓑ Ⓒ Ⓓ

39. Ⓐ Ⓑ Ⓒ Ⓓ

40. Ⓐ Ⓑ Ⓒ Ⓓ

Notes

Notes

Notes

Notes

Show What You Know® on the OAT for Grade 6, Additional Products

Student Workbook and Parent/Teacher Supplement for Mathematics

Flash Cards for Mathematics and Reading

**For more information, call our toll-free number: 1.877.PASSING (727.7464)
or visit our website: www.passtheoat.com**